Stories of Capitalism

Stories of Capitalism

INSIDE THE ROLE OF FINANCIAL ANALYSTS

Stefan Leins

The University of Chicago Press   Chicago and London

PUBLICATION OF THIS BOOK HAS BEEN AIDED BY GRANTS
FROM THE BEVINGTON FUND AND THE SWISS
NATIONAL SCIENCE FOUNDATION.

The University of Chicago Press, Chicago 60637
The University of Chicago Press, Ltd., London
© 2018 by The University of Chicago

Published 2018
Printed in the United States of America

27 26 25 24 23 22 21 20 19 18   1 2 3 4 5

ISBN-13: 978-0-226-52339-2 (cloth)
ISBN-13: 978-0-226-52342-2 (paper)
ISBN-13: 978-0-226-52356-9 (e-book)
DOI: 10.7208/chicago/9780226523569.001.0001

Library of Congress Cataloging-in-Publication Data
Names: Leins, Stefan, author.
Title: Stories of capitalism : inside the role of financial analysts / Stefan Leins.
Description: Chicago ; London : The University of Chicago Press, 2018. |
Includes bibliographical references and index.
Identifiers: LCCN 2017031750 | ISBN 9780226523392 (cloth : alk. paper) |
ISBN 9780226523422 (pbk. : alk. paper) | ISBN 9780226523569 (e-book)
Subjects: LCSH: Financial analysts | Financial services industry—Employees. |
Finance—Social aspects. | Investment banking—Social aspects—Switzerland. |
Banks and banking—Switzerland. | Business anthropology.
Classification: LCC HG4621 .L45 2018 | DDC 332.1—dc23
LC record available at https://lccn.loc.gov/2017031750

♾ This paper meets the requirements of ANSI/NISO Z39.48-1992
(Permanence of Paper)

Contents

Acknowledgments

The fieldwork for this study began long before I planned my actual research project. To finance my studies in anthropology, I spent several years working part-time in banks. The first bank I worked for, a French institution, has now become well known as the field site of Vincent Lépinay's *Codes of Finance* (2011). The second bank was a US bank in Zurich. I did not choose to work in banks because of a particular interest in financial markets. Rather, my decision was based on the fact that banks paid better salaries to working students than bars or archives did. From the very first day on the job, however, the cultural features of finance intrigued me. I remember the first time I dressed as a banker, participated in one of the drinking rituals, and experienced the feeling of finger-counting one million US dollars that a US client wanted to pick up in cash. These experiences were made possible by a number of banking practitioners who trusted me and allowed me to become familiar with their working environment.

Later, at Swiss Bank, the main observation site of my research, another group of bankers made it possible for me to do fieldwork inside the bank. I had the good fortune of being supervised by excellent mentors with a sincere interest in anthropology and in a critical assessment of current financial market activities. Furthermore, many of the financial analysts helped me by providing information, explaining their working routines, and allowing me to become part of their professional lives. Without these individuals, this research would not have been possible, and I gratefully acknowledge their support. It is common in ethnographies to omit the real names of these door openers and interlocutors. I trust that they will nevertheless be able to identify themselves.

My academic mentors, Peter Finke and Ellen Hertz, accompanied my research project from the beginning and substantially contributed to the completion of this book. I want to thank Peter for opening the doors to academia for me, for believing in my project, and for his ongoing support, academically as well as personally. Similarly, Ellen showed incredible support and shared her great expertise throughout the entire research and writing phase. It was Ellen's idea to send the manuscript to the University of Chicago Press—something I would probably not have dared to do. Thank you, Ellen! Heinz Käufeler also deserves my gratitude. As director of the Swiss Graduate School in Anthropology, he gave a whole generation of young researchers like me the chance to meet and discuss our research projects. In addition to that, Heinz was always there for an inspiring talk on anthropology and actually everything else, from daily politics to hipster culture.

Swiss Bank's research program funded the fieldwork phase of my project. The Forschungskredit of the University of Zurich provided financial support during the writing phase. Both these institutions allowed me to fully focus on my academic interests, while at the same time providing me with the financial means to do so. I thank everyone involved in the decision to fund this project.

While I worked on this project, many people helped to improve my study by sharing their comments and ideas. At the Department of Social Anthropology and Cultural Studies in Zurich, my colleagues contributed to my work through countless inspiring discussions and informal talks. As part of the Swiss Graduate School in Anthropology, Jean and John Comaroff, Aldo Haesler, George Marcus, Richard Rottenburg, and Heinzpeter Znoj commented on my project. At Goldsmiths, Rebecca Cassidy, Claire Loussouarn, Andrea Pisac, and Alex Preda provided useful input. In Jena, sociologists working with Oliver Kessler, Jens Maesse, and Hanno Pahl helped me to strengthen my line of argumentation. So did Karin Knorr Cetina, who commented on my research at a workshop held in Zurich in 2015. Carlo Caduff and Bill Maurer provided valuable comments on the original research outline. Sandra Bärnreuther read parts of my revised manuscript. And Emilio Marti was kind enough to read my introduction and theoretical discussion to check whether my line of argumentation made sense to a scholar from organization and management studies.

Laura Bear of the London School of Economics anthropology de-

ACKNOWLEDGMENTS [ix]

partment, where I spent two terms as a visiting researcher in 2015, was an invaluable mentor and provided a wealth of insightful comments on my study. She also coordinated the Programme on the Anthropology of Economy that gave me the opportunity to discuss my work with some of the world's leading economic anthropologists. I thank Ritu Birla, Maxim Bolt, Kimberly Chong, Elisabeth Ferry, Karen Ho, Caroline Humphrey, Deborah James, Stine Puri, Gisa Weszkalnys, and Caitlin Zaloom for their comments during the workshop on speculation that took place at LSE in May 2015. I also thank Juan Pablo Pardo-Guerra and Leon Wansleben, who offered their comments at various times.

Furthermore, I am indebted to the Zurich-based Economy and Culture reading group that met regularly to discuss the history of economic thought from Mandeville to Mankiw. As part of our curriculum, Nina Bandi, David Eugster, Dominik Gross, Michael Koller, and Julia Reichert read and commented on an early version of the book.

At the University of Chicago Press, Priya Nelson shared my enthusiasm for the book's topic and helped me turn my first manuscript into a readable and hopefully enjoyable book. I am indebted to Priya, the editorial board of the University of Chicago Press, and the manuscript's reviewers for believing in my book and helping me to improve it. Daromir Rudnyckyj, who agreed to reveal his identity, was one of the reviewers. His detailed and inspiring comments are now reflected in many parts of the book.

Last but not least, my family and friends provided me with unwavering support during my research and motivated me at times when it seemed hard to continue. I thank my mother Dominique and my father Thomas for their unconditional support and the great amount of love they have given me and my siblings, Miriam and Robin. Your beautiful ways of promoting creativity, curiosity, and open-mindedness have been the very foundation for this book. Finally, and above all, I owe my gratitude to Nadja Mosimann. Without your intellect, your passion, and your unparalleled personal support, none of this would have been possible. Thank you, Nadja—for no less than everything. This book is dedicated to you.

· 1 ·

Meeting the Predictors

In spring 2010, it seemed as if the financial crisis had come to an end. Governments had bailed out many of the so-called systemically relevant banks, and stock markets appeared to be slowly recovering. The tragic effects of the financial crisis were visible, however, in struggling industries and growing unemployment. Countries such as Greece and Spain reported youth unemployment rates of more than 50 percent, while at the same time governments lowered their spending to unprecedented levels. Furthermore, as a direct consequence of housing market speculation, approximately 10 million homeowners had lost their homes in the United States alone. Most financial market participants claimed, nevertheless, that the financial markets seemed to have overcome the crisis.

This optimistic view did not last long. On May 7, 2010, I was supposed to meet with a member of the financial analysis department I was aiming to study. At 9:12 a.m., my cell phone rang: "I don't know whether you've already seen it," the caller said, "but the markets are going crazy. I'm afraid we have to cancel our meeting."[1] I had no idea what the person was referring to, and so I went online to find out. It turned out that, at 2:45 p.m. New York time on May 6, the Dow Jones Industrial Average Index, one of the most important stock market benchmark indices, lost 9 percent of its value within a few minutes. Although the exact reasons for the Flash Crash, as this incident came to be known, have been subject to discussion ever since, one thing became clear to me that day: however legitimate they might look, financial market forecasts can become useless very quickly. In fact, predicting market developments is—as some financial analysts themselves like to say—often simply "betting on the future." The same insight ultimately applied to the long-term development of the overall financial crisis after this particular moment in 2010. Instead of experiencing the aftermath of the crisis, I became witness to the "currency wars" ("Currency Wars," 2010), an economy "on the edge" ("On the Edge," 2011), and what was almost the end of the euro ("Is This Really the End?" 2011). In other words, I observed the sad continuation of the biggest financial crisis since the Great Depression.

I joined Swiss Bank (a pseudonym I use throughout this book) in September 2010 for a two-year fieldwork phase because I wanted to understand what happens inside one of today's biggest black boxes: the banking world. I was born and raised in Zurich, the home of the two major Swiss banks, as well as dozens of small and medium-sized financial institutions. Even though Zurich is massively influenced by its financial sector, which contributes no less than 22 percent of the canton's GDP (Kanton Zürich 2011, 7), the sector has remained opaque to many of the people of Zurich. This opacity results partly from the fact that its employees rarely discuss their work in public. Also, Swiss banks have done a good job of presenting the banking sector as a simple service industry, rather than as a field of powerful corporate actors who heavily influence their host cities and dominate much of the world's economy.

The figures speak for themselves: In 2005, the total assets held in Swiss bank accounts were worth eight times Switzerland's GDP (in the United States, the total assets held on domestic accounts were approximately equal to the US GDP). These assets predominantly come from abroad, which makes Switzerland the world's largest offshore financial center. Roughly speaking, Swiss bank accounts contain a third of the world's financial wealth that is held abroad (Straumann 2006, 139; Wetzel, Flück, and Hofstätter 2010, 352; Zucman 2016).

With the consent of Swiss Bank, I was taking part in the day-to-day work life of the bank's financial analysis department, a large division of about 150 highly educated and well-paid employees. Financial analysts collect information and conduct analyses to understand current developments in financial markets. Then they valuate companies, business sectors, countries, and geographical regions to identify opportunities for investment. In so doing, they become powerful market actors. Their valuations and investment advice generate, increase, reduce, or cut short flows of capital. Companies can prosper if financial analysts see them as promising future investments. Countries can be flooded with foreign direct investment if analysts are positive about their future economic development. Similarly, analysts have the power to let companies and nations perish. Just think of countries such as Argentina or Greece, where "markets just could not wait," or of forced company restructurings caused by an "increase in market pressure." Financial analysts thus, to some extent, govern the economy. They take part in negotiating the value of companies, countries, currencies, and other entities that have been made investable and tradable in the current financial market economy.[2]

It would, of course, be easy to see financial analysts as the only true holders of power in financial markets. But, as I learned during my time at Swiss Bank, the story is not that simple. Despite their influence, the role of financial analysts is challenged on two levels. First, doing financial analysis does not fit well with some of the key assumptions of economic theory. Economic theorists express a great deal of skepticism about whether it is possible to "beat the market," that is, to come up with specific forecasts that result in an investment strategy that performs better than the overall stock market. Since Cowles (1933), economists have argued that correctly forecasting market developments is more the result of chance than of straightforward calculation and expertise. And since the rise of Chicago-style neoclassical economics—today's leading school of economic thought—the claim that market movements can be predicted has been contested even more fiercely.

In the 1960s and 1970s, well-known economists such as Paul Samuelson, Eugene Fama, and Burton Malkiel popularized the critique of forecasting within the neoclassical school of economic thought. In his book *A Random Walk down Wall Street*, Malkiel ([1973] 1985, 16) stated that "taken to its logical extreme, it [the random walk] means that a blindfolded monkey throwing darts at a newspaper's financial pages could select a portfolio that would do just as well as one carefully selected by experts." Malkiel's provocative claim was based on Samuelson's and Fama's formulation of the efficient market hypothesis (see Fama 1965, 1970; Samuelson 1965).[3] The efficient market hypothesis states that markets are *informationally efficient*, which means that expected changes in the stock price are so quickly reflected in the price that there is no room for financial analysts to forecast stock price developments for a longer period of time. As Fama says, the only way to forecast stock market developments in an efficient market is if a market participant possesses information that is not available to any other market participant. Since financial analysts cannot systematically access such insider information, neoclassical economists believe that the scope for predicting market developments is limited.

Second, the activity of financial analysts is significantly challenged by its empirical success or lack thereof. As I experienced during my time at Swiss Bank, financial analysts often fail to predict the correct future developments of financial markets. They fail to do so particularly because, even under the assumption that markets are not efficient, analysts still never know *which* elements of the information gathered will affect the financial market in *what* way. Scholars such as Working (1934), Kendall (1953), and Osborne (1959) empirically tested this issue of the analysts' uncertainty about future developments. They all came to the conclusion that, on average, financial analysts are largely unable to outperform the market.

This finding has been repeatedly illustrated not only in empirical finance studies, but also in the media. From 2003 to 2009, for example, the *Chicago Sun-Times* published annual stock market forecasts from "investment expert" Adam Monk. Adam was a capuchin monkey that, with a little help from his owner Bill Hoffmann, randomly pointed to five stocks listed in the financial section of a newspaper at the beginning of each year. The *Chicago Sun-Times* later jokingly promoted these stocks as "investment advice." In 2006, after Adam Monk had impressively kept up with the overall market development and had even beaten many of his human colleagues, Jim Cramer, a well-known analyst with the television network CNBC, challenged Adam Monk. By also picking five stocks at the beginning of the year, Jim Cramer wanted to show how he—the star analyst—could outperform the monkey. He failed to prove his point: in 2006 and in 2008, the monkey managed to beat Cramer (performance tracked by *Free by 50* 2009). The same experiment was repeated in Great Britain, where Orlando, a ginger cat, outperformed human investors in 2012. Betting against a group of financial professionals and a group of novice students, Orlando generated the highest financial return of the three teams ("Investments" 2013).

Why Are There Financial Analysts?

The question that arises from these theoretical claims and empirical experiments is why there are financial analysts at all. In this book, I seek to explore the role of financial analysts and financial analysis as a market practice from an anthropological perspective. I am interested in how financial analysts act under conditions of uncertainty, how they construct their market forecasts, and how they become powerful market actors even if their practices are not plenary backed by economic theory and empirical success.

I argue that financial analysts establish and maintain their influential position in three ways. First, they are successful in presenting themselves as a group of market experts and, as such, as a distinct subprofessional category in banking. They distinguish themselves from other bankers by using cultural codes such as a particular language and style of dress and by referring to a particular body of acquired knowledge (see Boyer 2005, 2008). They thus acquire symbolic capital (Bourdieu 1984) that helps them to become recognized as a distinct and legitimate group of experts in finance. Second, by establishing market forecasts, analysts produce narratives that create a sense of agency in the highly unstable and uncertain field of financial markets. Their investment narratives[4] allow investors to believe that, rather than being random, market movements can be understood through the work of financial analysts. Third, financial analysts are market intermediaries whose existence and activities are helpful to wealth managers and the host bank. By constructing investment narratives, they allow wealth managers to pass narratives on to investors. Also, analysts help the bank gain commissions by continually encouraging its clients to invest. Overall, I argue that all these factors help financial analysts transform the skepticism of economic theory and experienced failure into a powerful market position.

Throughout this book, I use the term "financial analysts" or "analysts" to refer to *fundamental financial analysts* in particular.[5] Fundamental analysis is a market practice that aims to valuate stocks, bonds, and other financial market products on the basis of underlying financial data (such as a company's earnings, sales, or cash flow) and macroeconomic data (such as the development of interest rates or growth estimates). Fundamental analysts build on the assumption that analyzing financial and macroeconomic data can allow analysts to estimate a company's "intrinsic value," which, unlike its market value, contains all relevant information available to market participants and is not blurred by short-term biases (see Chiapello 2015, 19–20). By comparing the intrinsic value to the market value, analysts then predict future market movements. If the intrinsic value is higher than the current market value, analysts assume the stock price will rise (as information will eventually be reflected in the market value). If the intrinsic value is below the market value, analysts assume the stock price will fall (Bodie, Kane, and Marcus 2002; Copeland, Koller, and Murrin 2000; Zuckerman 2012).

Fundamental financial analysis is one particular style of doing financial analysis. Another style is technical analysis, sometimes also referred to as "chartism" (see Preda 2007, 2009; Zaloom 2003). Rather than looking at financial and economic data (financial analysts usually call them market fundamentals), technical analysts study the visual representation of the market price. Analyzing how the market prices of stocks, bonds, or other financial products develop over time, they try to recognize (visual) patterns that could give insights into how the price might develop in the future (see chapters 4 and 5 for detailed discussions of fundamental and technical analysis). What's important for now is that both fundamental and technical analysts lack legitimacy in neoclassical economic theory and experience failure in their everyday work. Their ways of dealing with failure, however, may be different. When talking about the construction of narrative strategies that help to overcome uncertainty, I am referring to fundamental analysis and not to chartism.

Financial Analysts and the Narrative Economy

I understand financial markets as a field in which single groups of market participants strive for influence and try to become members of respected subprofessional categories. This is, of course, not an entirely new approach. Since Marx, political economists have analyzed the economy as a field of political struggle. Similarly, economic anthropologists have long focused on the interplay between markets and power (see Hann and Hart 2011 for an overview). The "social studies of finance," however, an academic field that has inspired many of the studies to which I refer throughout this book, has so far paid little attention to the broader social and political role of financial experts. By highlighting the question of how knowledge is produced and circulated, scholars of the social studies of finance have predominantly examined financial market settings with a narrow focus on expert knowledge, rather than on how this expert knowledge becomes influential.

Many of the scholars investigating the relationship between knowledge and finance have adopted a particularly strong focus on the concept of *performativity*. Introduced by Michel Callon (1998), the term has been used to describe the framing of the economy (as a field) by economic theory. In his seminal article "What Does It Mean to Say That Economics Is Performative?" Callon (2007, 322) states, "To predict economic agents' behaviors, an economic theory does not have to be true; it simply needs to be believed by everyone." For Callon, the model of the market based on neoclassical economic assumptions—that is, efficient and entirely based on supply and demand—is not something that should be perceived as natural. Rather, it should be seen as a model that has become part of reality through an ongoing performative discourse, that is, a discourse that "contributes to the construction of a reality that it describes" (Callon 2007, 316; see also Muniesa 2014).[6]

To illustrate the focal points of such performative effects, scholars from the social studies of finance usually refer to two empirical examples. The first one is Garcia-Parpet's (2007) study of the strawberry market. Garcia-Parpet studied the restructuring of a French strawberry market, in which an economic adviser had an enormous impact on reframing the market setting according to neoclassical economic theory. Through architectural and technological interventions, the strawberry market began working according to economic theory not because economic theory is a natural law, but because people structured the market according to the neoclassical paradigm. The second example is that of the Black-Scholes formula. As MacKenzie and Millo (2003) have shown, the invention of formulas such as the Black-Scholes formula—a mathematical formula used for option pricing—have had a significant impact on the pricing models used in financial markets. In contrast to Garcia-Parpet's strawberry case, performativity is not enforced by architecture, technological innovation, and consulting, but rather by a kind of nonhuman agency of economic models designed according to the neoclassical paradigm (for an overview of contributions to economic performativity studies, see MacKenzie, Muniesa, and Siu 2007).

In many ways, the idea of performativity in finance has been important for groundbreaking and inspiring research and has helped to popularize the social studies of finance. An increasing number of scholars, however, have begun to take a critical view of the theory of performativity as put forward by Callon. Judith Butler (2010), for example, raised concerns that performativity, as used by scholars in the social studies of finance, tacitly reproduces the notion of economics as an autonomous field. Butler argues that if all economic processes are understood as being performed by economic theory, a critical analysis of its political dimension (apart from the hegemonic position of neoclassical economics) becomes difficult. Instead of "abandoning the critical position," as Callon suggests (Barry and Slater 2002, 301), Butler calls for an "effort to evaluate and oppose those multivalent operations of capitalism that augment income disparities, presume the functional necessity of poverty, and thwart efforts to establish just forms for the redistribution of wealth" (Butler 2010, 153).

Similarly, Philip Mirowski and Edward Nik-Khah (2007) have criticized the concept of performativity as having worrisome depoliticizing effects. They claim that scholars working on performativity believe and repeat the economists' stories as they are told among economists, rather than critically reflecting on them. In so doing, the authors argue, they have become companions of neoclassical economics, reproducing economic science as *quasi*-natural science. Criticism has also been formulated from an empirical perspective. In his book on expert knowledge in foreign exchange markets, Wansleben (2013a) argues that market knowledge is produced and framed by "epistemic cultures," rather than by economic theory (see also Knorr-Cetina 2007, 2011). Riles (2010) produced a similar critique based on observations of how legal scholars build up expertise in financial markets. Finally, anthropologist Daniel Miller (2002) critiques the performativity assumption by empirically showing that, contrary to the claims of economic textbooks and performativity scholars alike, "contemporary exchange rarely if ever works according to the laws of the market" (218).

In contrast to Miller, I believe economic theory to be an important influence on current market practices. Unlike the results from previous performativity studies, however, my study looks at a particular case in which an influential market practice has emerged and persisted *even though* it does not have a theoretical legitimacy in economics. One thing that probably explains this lack of performative effects between theory and practice in the case of financial analysis is that it is not a highly automated market practice. The estimation of the intrinsic value is based not only on calculative strategies, but also on culturally embedded interpretations and social interactions. This is significantly different from quantitative finance—or mathematical finance, as it is sometimes called—in which models directly influence investment decisions (often without a human intermediary who evaluates the outcome of the models). It is thus not surprising that many of the recent empirical studies on performativity have been conducted in the field of quantitative finance, such as portfolio pricing or algorithmic trading (see Beunza and Stark 2004; MacKenzie 2006; MacKenzie et al. 2012; MacKenzie and Millo 2003; Stark and Beunza 2009). In less automated areas, such as financial analysis, the relationship between economic theory and market practices differs. Financial analysts sometimes ignore or reject the concepts of economic theory, while at other times they use them to legitimize elements of their market practice. Here, economic theory is an important point of reference but does not perform market practices as is the case in quantitative finance.

Still, there is a lot to be learned from former research conducted in the social studies of finance, particularly when thinking about how expert knowledge emerges and how it is stabilized. Here, the work of Beunza and Garud is of critical importance. Beunza and Garud (2007) wrote a research article on financial analysts, which I discuss in various parts of my book. Having studied reports written by analysts, Beunza and Garud introduced the notion of financial analysts as creators of calculative frames. These calculative frames refer to the cognitive and material infrastructure of economic calculation and represent the way in which analysts accord meaning to information. Seeing financial analysts as frame makers creates scope for incorporating economic concepts, sociotechnical arrangements, and issues of cognition into analyses of analysts. In so doing, Beunza and Garud refine earlier ideas about analysts (that they are calculators, imitators, information processors, etc.) in order to tackle the complex field in which financial analysts operate.

What is missing in the research of Beunza and Garud is, however, an empirical observation of how these frames emerge on a practical level and how they become influential. The answer to this is part of the more general claim of my book: analysts become successful through the formulation of their forecasts as persuasive stories. Market predictions thus highly depend on the ability of the analysts to put them into a narrative structure.

Douglas Holmes and Arjun Appadurai, two leading anthropologists, have recently published books in which they stress this central role of language and narration in the current economy. In *Economy of Words: Communicative Imperatives in Central Banks*, Holmes (2014, 5) argues that markets are a "function of language." Analyzing the role and strategies of central banks, especially since the beginning of the financial crisis, he shows how communicative acts are responsible for creating what we understand as markets. The communication of central bank representatives, he claims, *makes* markets, rather than only describing or reacting to them. Readers may have noticed that this line of argumentation shows some similarities with the performativity thesis discussed above. In Holmes's analysis of the communicative strategies of central bank representatives, however, performative effects take place between market practitioners and the market itself. It is thus not primarily economic theory that performs the activity of central bankers, but central bankers that perform the market through utterances. When we think of the role of the European Central Bank during the crisis of the euro or the strategy of Janet Yellen in recent monetary policy strategy, the role of such utterances becomes apparent. As Holmes (2009; 2014, 11) convincingly shows, narratives have become a "main tool of monetary policy" in the current market environment.

In *Banking on Words: The Failure of Language in the Age of Derivative Finance*, Appadurai (2016) similarly highlights the role of language in current financial markets. Drawing on the claim that derivatives— that is, financial instruments whose values derive from other assets— have become a central tool of speculation since the beginning of the 2000s, he analyzes the financial crisis that started in 2007 in the context of language. A derivative, to Appadurai, is "a promise about the uncertain future" (2). The fact that a promise is a linguistic act makes the derivatives market a linguistic phenomenon. Unlike Holmes, Appadurai diagnoses a recent failure, rather than a success, of language in finance. Following his line of argumentation, the breakdown of the derivatives market in 2007 that marked the beginning of the financial crisis was in fact a breakdown of a "chain of promises."

The work of Holmes and Appadurai helps us to think about language and narration as a critical quality of the current economy. Narratives, in the financial market context, entail elements that arise from affect, calculative approaches, and tacit knowledge, as well as from embodied experience.[7] They are constructed through performance, aesthetics, and senses of ethical order. Although these narratives are usually implicit, they can be made explicit when analysts spell out market reports or investment recommendations and communicate them to other financial market participants.

A number of anthropologists have elaborated on this multitude of components that contribute to such narratives. In her work on traders, Zaloom (2003, 2006, 2009) has stressed the role of affect and the embodiment of experience. As she points out, in financial markets, "affect arises when knowledge has no solid ground" (Zaloom 2009, 245). She, as well as Lépinay and Hertz (2005), illustrate how market participants develop affective relations to the market in order to cope with the unknowable future. The same is true for the financial analysts I studied. They actively claim that in order to become a good analyst, one has to develop a "market feeling." This "market feeling" is the result of embodied experiences of past success and failure, which is then extrapolated to future hopes and doubts and, once it is stabilized, becomes a conviction (see Chong and Tuckett 2015; Miyazaki 2007; Wansleben 2013a).

Parallel to the establishment of a "market feeling," financial analysts engage in calculative approaches. Because there is not a single calculative approach that promises superior outcome, these calculative approaches also are only part of a broad repertoire of techniques that contribute to the overall narrative. Analysts can choose between various approaches to derive price predictions. These calculative approaches are, however, never used without the reconciliation of their results with the perspective on the future that derives from affect. In situations in which the "gut feeling" (an affective element) and calculative outcome differ in substantial ways, analysts often prefer affect to calculation.

Also, investment narratives are constructed through performance and aesthetics. Here, the work of Riles (2006, 2011) is of considerable importance. In her research, Riles shows how legal documents aesthetically contribute to financial market narratives, which is a process that can similarly be observed when studying the construction of narratives among financial analysts. Analysts work with persuasive charts, tables, and illustrations to construct new or stabilize existing narratives.

Because of the central function of language and narration in financial markets, I propose to think about the current economy as a *narrative economy*.[8] To understand this concept, it is crucial to see that the economy today is a system directed toward the future. As Beckert (2013, 2016) states, all the characteristic elements of current capitalism are built on expectations. Innovation, credit, commodification, and competition, which are the four characteristic elements according to Beckert, are all market practices that involve a management of expectations. Because this management of expectations requires "imaginaries of the future" (Beckert 2013, 328; see also Bear 2015, 2016; Comaroff and Comaroff 2000; Guyer 2007), they are practices taking place under conditions of uncertainty. This also is true of financial analysts and their attempts to predict market movements. Analysts have to create imaginaries of the future to cope with the uncertainty they are facing.

In a narrative economy, such imaginaries of the future become a central tool of resource allocation. Hence, the current economy can be understood as a system that thrives on imagination and narration. Here, the role of financial analysts becomes apparent: They are the creators of narratives of the future, which are then used by other market participants when allocating financial resources.

.   .   .

Why do financial analysts exist in the market? In this book, I seek anthropological answers to this question that economists have failed to resolve. I first elaborate on the relationship between economic theory and forecasting as a market practice. After a brief look into why market forecasting has long been problematic for economic theory, I turn to the life inside the bank. I look at the way financial analysts present themselves as a subprofessional category and how they distinguish themselves from other groups in banking. I use these ethnographic descriptions to demonstrate that, in order to become influential, analysts depend heavily on the notion that bankers are not a homogeneous group but a conglomerate of various subprofessional groups with distinct self-ascriptions that are in ongoing competition for legitimacy and influence.

After that, I focus on the market practices in which financial analysts engage and on the way they construct investment narratives. Here, the focus shifts from the analysts as *actors* to analysis as *action*. By describing the approaches that analysts use, I show that financial analysis is a market practice that fluctuates between calculative approaches and cultural interpretations. Last, I turn to the role of financial analysts as market intermediaries. Here, I leave the financial analysis department and try to grasp the relationships between financial analysts and other groups of actors in finance. I describe how market forecasts are circulated in the bank and how they are used by other stakeholders to decide how money should be invested. I address the fact that, despite usually being presented as neutral observers and interpreters of the market, analysts have an active role in promoting investments.

We will see that financial analysts play a critical role in producing visions of "the economy" and its future development. As experts in financial markets, they create imaginary future scenarios that enable other financial market participants to speculate on the rise or fall of stock prices, the success or failure of particular investment products, and the growth or decline of entire national economies. The practices they employ to derive these narratives are sometimes reminiscent of techniques of divination, as they have been described by classic anthropologists such as Evans-Pritchard (1937) or Turner (1975). As Comaroff and Comaroff (2000) remind us, this is a surprising but characteristic feature of how capitalism in its neoliberal form materializes in everyday ethics and practices. Speculation, they state, is a new form of "enchantment" (310). It feeds on imaginaries of the future and on the notion that through the anticipation of the future, wealth can be created without much effort. With this in mind, this book can be read as a description of a particular form of enchantment fostered by neo-liberal capitalism. It reveals that rather than representing a disputable practice, the work of financial analysts is at the heart of today's financial market economy and a characterizing feature of its neoliberal culture.

· 2 ·

The Problem with Forecasting in Economic Theory

Much of the recent work in the social studies of finance has focused on the relationship between economics as an academic discipline and the economy as a field. When thinking about the relationship between theory and practice, one of three positions is usually taken. First, one can argue that economic theory *reflects* practice, which is a position that most economists unfamiliar with the social studies of finance adopt. Second, one can claim that theory *performs* practice, which is the key message of the performativity approach I introduced in chapter 1. Third, one can argue that economic theory and practice are not linked by much of a relationship at all. This is the point made by scholars studying markets as epistemic cultures (Knorr Cetina 2007, 2011; Wansleben 2013a) or as an ideological project (Carrier 1997, Miller 2002).

In terms of financial analysis, however, none of these positions accurately explains the relationship between economic theory and financial analysis as a market practice. First, if economic theory were an accurate reflection of the economy as a field, there should be a theoretical explanation for the existence of financial analysis. As we will see in the following, such an explanation does not exist. Second, if economic theory generally performed the economy as a field, financial analysis should not exist, for mainstream economists claim that there is no theoretical foundation to stock market forecasting. Hence, financial analysis seems to work outside the boundary conditions of the performativity theory. Third, if economic theory and economic practice could be seen as two fully separable fields, there would be no reason for financial analysts to actually refer to economic theory as much as they do. Authors of practical textbooks on financial analysis and practicing analysts, however, still put some effort into theorizing their market practice as economically meaningful. Economic theory is thus used as a point of reference in financial analysis, even though, in the case of market forecasting, the relationship between theory and practice is problematic and prone to conflict. This is not only true for neoclassical economic theory, which is the dominant school of thought in economics as it is practiced within and outside the academy today, but also for behavioral economics and new institutional economics—the two schools of thought that gained prominence by criticizing Chicago-style neoclassical economics after it gained popularity in the 1970s.

Neoclassical Economics

Neoclassical economics, today's mainstream economic school of thought, dates back to the end of the nineteenth century. It became the dominant school of thought in the middle of the twentieth century, when a number of economists at the University of Chicago transformed the discipline of economics in significant ways (Lee 2009). Prior to the 1950s, the discipline of economics was already popular and widespread. As Harvie, Lightfoot, and Weir (2013) and Jensen and Smith (1984) argue, however, economics at the time was dominated by single empirical case studies and ad hoc theories. The introduction of a systematic approach linked to fundamental convictions about how markets work enabled the Chicago School of Economics to shape economics in a particular way and made the neoclassical school of thought the dominant approach in economics (Van Horn and Mirowski 2010; Van Overtveldt 2007).

In 1962 political economist H. Laurence Miller first identified the characteristics of this new and distinct kind of economics from Chicago that became so powerful within a short time. In the article "On the 'Chicago School of Economics,'" he writes:

What does distinguish him [the economist from Chicago] from other economists are a number of closely related attributes: the polar position that he occupies among economists as an advocate of an individualistic market economy; the emphasis that he puts on the usefulness and relevance of [. . .] neoclassical economic theory; the way in which he equates the actual and the ideal market; the way in which he sees and applies economics in and to every nook and cranny of life; and the emphasis that he puts on hypothesis-testing as a neglected element in the development of positive economics. (Miller 1962, 65)

As Miller observes, scholars such as Milton Friedman, Gary Becker, and Eugene Fama, who were all affiliated with the University of Chicago in the 1950s and 1960s, developed economics in a much more systematic, applicable, and normative way. In terms of how markets work, the new liberal economists from Chicago were heavily influenced by classic liberal economists such as Adam Smith and David Ricardo, who described markets as being governed by an invisible hand that regulates the supply and demand of economic goods without intervention.[1] But the members of the Chicago School of Economics lived in a very different time from that of their predecessors. Having experienced World War II and the emergence of the first socialist states, they argued that self-governed markets have to be actively promoted by a reformulation of the role of the state and backed by a more systematic (neoclassical) economic science (Friedman 1962; Friedman and Friedman 1990). This line of argumentation was based on the writings of political philosopher Friedrich A. Hayek (1944, 1960), who claimed that individual economic freedom was the key factor in preventing the "tyranny of central planning" that, in Hayek's eyes, played a crucial role in Germany under the Nazi regime and in socialist states.

The assumption that state regulations and interventions mean that free markets do not naturally exist and need to be *naturalized* by active intervention led to the political program that many social scientists (though only few economists) today refer to as neoliberalism.[2] The close link between a new systematic way of establishing economic theory and the aim of producing politically applicable results helped the neoclassical school of thought gain influence within the discipline of economics and beyond.

After the 1970s, neoclassical economics became the leading paradigm in economics and also influenced the subfield of corporate finance in significant ways. The introductory textbook *The Modern Theory of Corporate Finance* (Jensen and Smith 1984) impressively demonstrates that the success of neoclassical economics provided a new paradigm for the study of finance. In the third sentence of the introduction to the book, the authors state, "Corporate financial theory prior to the 1950s was riddled with logical inconsistencies and was almost totally prescriptive, that is, normatively oriented" (2). In promoting a *modern* theory of corporate finance, Jensen and Smith identified five concepts as theoretical cornerstones: the efficient market hypothesis, the portfolio theory, the capital asset pricing theory, the option pricing theory, and the agency theory.[3]

In the context of financial analysis, the efficient market hypothesis is of particular interest. It states that markets are informationally efficient, which means that all information that is publicly available about a company is instantly reflected in a company's stock price, making it impossible to predict stock market movements in the long run.

Although the efficient market hypothesis was coined as such by the members of the Chicago School of Economics, an efficient market hypothesis *avant la lettre* can be traced back to the nineteenth century (Jovanovic and Le Gall 2001; Preda 2004).[4] Furthermore, in 1933 Alfred Cowles published a paper that empirically tested the attempt to forecast stock market price developments. After having analyzed 7,500 stock market forecasts from sixteen financial service agencies, Cowles came to the conclusion that "Statistical tests of the best individual records failed to demonstrate that they exhibited skill, and indicated that they more probably were results of chance" (Cowles 1933, 323). To show that this lack of success was not due to the poor work of individual unskilled analysts, Cowles also tested the success of the predictions published by William Peter Hamilton, editor of the *Wall Street Journal* at that time. In his paper, Cowles concludes

> William Peter Hamilton, editor of the *Wall Street Journal*, publishing forecasts of the stock market based on the Dow Theory over a period of 26 years, from 1904 to 1929, inclusive, achieved a result better than what would ordinarily be regarded as a normal investment return, but poorer than the result of a continuous outright investment in representative common stocks for this period. On 90 occasions he announced changes in the outlook for the market. Forty-five of these predictions were successful and 45 unsuccessful. (Cowles 1933, 323; italics in the original)

This devastating result, published in *Econometrica*'s first volume in the article "Can Stock Market Forecasters Forecast?," was one of the first empirical studies that problematized the predictability of stock market developments in a systematic way. On a practical level, however, the study did not change much about the increasing popularity of stock market forecasts. On the contrary, the use of forecasts as a market technique actually grew substantially at the end of the 1930s. As Wansleben (2012, 251–55) points out, one reason for this trend was the changing regulatory environment ushered in by President Roosevelt's New Deal. Because economists linked to Roosevelt argued that the Great Depression was partly caused by investors having insufficient information on how companies were performing, companies were made to comply with new reporting standards that provided more information on their business activities and financial situation. The huge amount of new information helped financial analysts expand their role as interpreters of market information.

On an academic level, the testing of stock market forecasts was repeated several times between the 1930s and 1960s. As publications by Working (1934), Kendall (1953), and Osborne (1959) show, these later tests confirmed Cowles's result by demonstrating that stock market prices behaved randomly rather than predictably. But it was only after the birth of what was called modern finance in Chicago that criticisms of forecasting became a central issue in economics.

From the 1960s onward, leading economists Paul Samuelson and Eugene Fama retested and wrote papers opposing the assumption that historical developments or mispriced information can be used to predict stock market developments. In 1965 Samuelson published "Proof That Properly Anticipated Prices Fluctuate Randomly." In the article, he tested the development of wheat prices traded in Chicago and came to the conclusion that the fluctuation of the prices represented a normal distribution. Proceeding from his conclusion, Samuelson described the development of the wheat prices he studied as a random walk—in other words, a movement that cannot be predicted.

In the same year, and apparently independently from Samuelson (Lo 2008), Fama published "The Behavior of Stock-Market Prices" (1965), in which he also elaborated on the occurrence of random walks (a term borrowed from statistics) in stock markets:

> [T]he theory of random walks says that the future path of the price
> level of a security is no more predictable than the path of a series
> of cumulated random numbers. In statistical terms the theory

says that successive price changes are independent, identically distributed random variables. Most simply this implies that the series of price changes has no memory, that is, the past cannot be used to predict the future in any meaningful way. (Fama 1965, 34)

As the cited section shows, Fama uses the random walk theory to debunk attempts by technical analysts to recognize visual patterns in the historical development of stock prices and use them to predict future developments. Before he introduces the random walk theory, Fama writes that "Although there are many different chartist [i.e., technical analysis] theories, they all make the same basic assumption. That is, they all assume that the past behavior of a security's price is rich in information concerning its future behavior" (34).

Unlike technical analysts, fundamental analysts identify price discrepancies between a company's intrinsic value and market value, which are caused by unpriced or mispriced information (see chapter 5 in this volume). This means that their practice could have been legitimate even under the assumption that visual patterns are not replicated over time. Fama's development of what he later termed "the efficient market hypothesis," however, represented an attack on both technical and fundamental analysis. In a later article, Fama makes his position very clear when he writes that the primary role

of the capital market is allocation of ownership of the economy's capital stock. In general terms, the ideal is a market in which prices provide accurate signals for resource allocation: that is, a market in which firms can make production-investment decisions, and investors can choose among the securities that represent ownership of firms' activities under the assumption that security prices at any time "fully reflect" all available information. A market in which prices always "fully reflect" available information is called "efficient." (Fama 1970, 383)

After reviewing a number of empirical studies, Fama comes to the conclusion that his definition of an ideal (i.e., efficient) market is not simply wishful thinking. He states, "The evidence in support of the efficient market model is extensive, and [. . .] contradictory evidence is sparse" (Fama 1970, 416). Reviewing *weak* tests (considering historical price data), *semistrong* tests (considering publicly available data), and *strong* tests (considering monopolistic access to information), Fama concludes that testing on all three levels suggests that security prices fully reflect all available information *at any point*.[5] In terms of financial analysis, this means that a fundamental analyst has no chance of systematically detecting unpriced information that will be reflected in the market price at some stage in the future. The logic of efficient markets indicates that, as Samuelson (1965, 41) says, "If one could be sure that the price will rise, it would already have risen."

Soon after the formulation of the efficient market hypothesis, criticism arose among a number of economists who did not agree with the underlying assumptions of the hypothesis. As Fama (1970) himself said, his claim that markets are efficient was based on the assumption that, first, market actors form expectations about future price developments rationally and, second, markets in general evolve toward an equilibrium, that is, a situation in which economic forces of supply and demand lead to a temporarily stable pricing of a traded good (Lo 2008).

These two assumptions, which are still at the center of neoclassical economics today, were soon challenged by two economic schools of thought that began gaining popularity in the 1970s: behavioral economics and new institutional economics. Both schools of thought challenge the neoclassical assumptions of unconfined rational actors and efficient markets. Behavioral economists use insights gained from psychology to make their point; new institutional economists refer to political economy to undergird their criticism.

Behavioral Economics

Behavioral economics, as the name implies, studies the behavior of individuals when making economic decisions. Historically, the focus on economic behavior can be traced back to Adam Smith's *Theory of Moral Sentiments* ([1759] 2002), in which Smith elaborated on the ethical and psychological foundations of economic action. As Cartwright (2011, 5) states, however, the significance of ethics and psychology in the study of economic action was derogated in the study of economics at the end of the nineteenth century by Alfredo Pareto, who insisted that economics should focus on describing what economic actors empirically do, rather than on asking *why* they do it. In the 1960s, however, as a reaction to the increasing institutionalization of neoclassical economics and its assumption-based modeling of markets, a number of scholars started thinking about the psychological foundations of economic behavior again.

The revival of the study of economic behavior in terms of psychological phenomena was mainly driven by the seminal work of Herbert Simon, Daniel Kahneman, and Amos Tversky. Simon was the first economist to question the ability of market actors to act rationally. As he argued, economic actors want to act rationally but their ability to do so is bounded by their limited access to information and by the uncertainty that surrounds future events (Simon 1957). Even though many of today's behavioral economists count Simon as one of the founding fathers of their school of thought, his new line of argumentation was more institutional than behavioral. I will therefore come back to Simon's concept of bounded rationality when discussing new institutional economics.

Kahneman and Tversky, on the other hand, built their critique of the assumption of rational actors on insights gained from psychological behavioral studies and introduced them into economics. They argued that, in addition to bounded information and uncertainty, heuristics and cognitive biases also prevent market actors from acting rationally, as they lead to systematic errors in decision-making processes (Kahneman and Tversky 1973, 1979). One example that is usually used to illustrate such errors is the existence of risk aversion. If a person is given the choice of entering a lottery with a 50 percent chance of winning either US$1,000 or nothing (option A) or receiving US$450 with no risk attached (option B), most people choose option B, even though the average return is statistically higher for option A. According to Kahneman and Tversky, people thus tend to avoid risk if they can, even though, from the perspective of maximizing benefit, it would make more sense to pick the option attached to risk. In addition to risk aversion, Kahneman and Tversky introduced and tested a number of other heuristics and cognitive biases to show that, empirically, people often do not act in the rational way assumed by neoclassical economic theory (Kahneman 2011 offers a good overview of further empirical examples).

Although the work of Kahneman and Tversky is often used today to claim that human decision making is irrational, such a conclusion actually is false. Kahneman, Tversky, and many other behavioral economists do not fundamentally challenge the notion of rationality, but rather look for heuristics and biases that prevent economic actors from acting rationally. Like Simon, they say that actors *aim* to act rationally but their rationality is limited by the existence of constraints. This loose alignment with models that presume humans to act rationally is probably the reason why the work of John Maynard Keynes, who also frequently referred to the psychology of market behavior, is rarely ever mentioned in the work of behavioral economists (one exception is the work of Akerlof and Shiller 2009). Keynes's (1936) notion of animal spirits in *The General Theory of Employment, Interest, and Money* represented a much more fundamental attack on the assumption that economic actors act rationally and thus proved to be harder to integrate into rational choice theory than the findings of behavioral economists.

Behavioral finance recently became a particularly popular subfield of behavioral economics. It focuses explicitly on economic behavior in a financial market context. As in behavioral economics, behavioral finance starts with the assumption that "a few psychological phenomena pervade the entire landscape of finance" (Shefrin 2000, 4). Behavioral finance is of particular interest to my study because, apart from applying concepts from behavioral economics to investment decision making, a number of scholars active in this field have explicitly addressed the role of heuristics and biases in financial analysis.

Montier (2002), for example, lists a variety of biases and heuristics that investors and analysts should be careful of when engaging in investment or valuation processes. The concepts of overoptimism and overconfidence, for example, refer to the fact that market actors tend to think of themselves as being more capable of interpreting the markets than other market actors. Cognitive dissonance describes the tendency of market actors to deny that they made wrong assumptions when they are presented with facts that contradict those assumptions. Confirmation bias and conservatism bias point to similar phenomena. They both characterize the phenomenon that once market actors have chosen a strategy, they primarily seek to preserve that strategy by searching for data that confirm rather than challenge it.

Such biases can indeed be observed when studying the work of financial analysts. When thinking about the role of market forecasting, however, being aware that cognitive biases exist does not help to legitimize the market practice of making future predictions. This is because in a biased market environment it hardly helps to be unbiased, since the market price will reflect those biases. An analyst would thus have to anticipate specific biased decisions made by other market actors in order to come up with market forecasts that benefit from the existence of such biases.

This issue is only partly acknowledged, however, by scholars active in the field of behavioral finance. On the one hand, they claim that decision making is biased and thus markets cannot be understood as being efficient. On the other hand, some scholars claim that by taking such biases into account, investors and analysts can estimate the unbiased value of a stock, a bond, or another financial product (see, for example, Michaely and Womack 2005; Shefrin 2000, 33–58). This claim is based on the erroneous assumption that biases are temporarily limited and will, at some point in the future, be adjusted. But if one acknowledges that market prices reflect biases and heuristics in the present, it is illogical to assume that markets will at some stage in the future depict an unbiased value that an analyst can estimate in advance. It is interesting that financial analysts often make the same error. They assume that although current prices are driven by manipulation and psychological excess, future prices can be predicted by fact-based estimations.

Apart from some of these more practically oriented scholars, however, behavioral economics does not provide a theory-based justification of financial analysis. Because behavioral economists consider market actors to be biased and acting on heuristics, their view means that successful market forecasting is as impossible as it is assumed to be in neoclassical economic theory. In a recent interview with the magazine *Time*, ("10 Questions" 2011), Kahneman made his position very clear and even referred to Malkiel's monkey metaphor, which is usually used by radical defenders of the efficient market hypothesis. Asked whether to trust financial market experts and their instincts, Kahneman answered, "There are domains in which expertise is not possible. Stock picking is a good example. And in long-term [. . .] forecasting, it's been shown that experts are just not better than a dice-throwing monkey."

New Institutional Economics

New institutional economics is the second economic school of thought that gained popularity as an alternative to neoclassical economics in the 1970s. Like behavioral economics, new institutional economics criticizes neoclassical economics for its assumptions that economic actors can be modeled as unconfined rational actors and that markets generally produce efficient equilibria operating on supply and demand. Unlike behavioral economists, however, new institutional economists do not limit their critique to psychological phenomena. They also foreground the role played by the distribution and cost of information and the asymmetric power relations between economic actors.

As the name implies, new institutional economics is particularly concerned with the notion that institutions have played no role in the postwar neoclassical paradigm (Furubotn and Richter 2005, 1; North 1992, 3). In economics, institutions are defined as the social rules, norms, and conventions that structure the way people interact. They emerge from culturally embedded ideas and ideologies (Hodson 2006, 2; North 1990, 3; 1992). Economists in the institutional tradition agree that institutions influence human behavior by either constraining or promoting it. In both cases, they structure how people behave and interact with others. In the late nineteenth and early twentieth century, institutions were still considered relevant in many economic analyses (see, for example, Coase 1937; Commons 1924; Veblen [1899] 2007), but the acknowledgment of the existence of institutions disappeared with the rise of Chicago-style neoclassical economics.

The claim that institutions matter, as economist Douglass North (1990) explained, became a remarkable counterargument to the modeling of economic actors as unbiased and having free and unlimited access to information. Because institutions are understood as being culturally embedded social conventions, the new institutional approach also paved the way for scholars outside economics to think about (economic) behavior and interaction. Soon, scholars of sociology (see all contributions in Brinton and Nee 1998), political science (see Hall and Taylor 1996), and anthropology (see Acheson 1994; Ensminger 1992; Finke 2005, 2014) joined the debate surrounding the foundations of human (economic) behavior. This broad range of influence led to the situation that we have today, in which many forms of new institutionalisms exist. In terms of the relationship between economic theory and financial analysis as a market practice, however, three thematic clusters are of particular relevance: the limits of rationality, the concept of transaction costs, and the critique of the neoclassical concept of market equilibrium.

I mentioned that Herbert Simon's work heavily influenced new institutional economics. Unlike mainstream economists, Simon argued that the rationality of economic actors is bounded by their limited access to information and the uncertainty of future developments. North (1990) argues that these informational constraints and the ubiquity of uncertainty are the reasons institutions are built. Such constraints help economic actors create a certain degree of stability and predictability of possible outcomes when interacting (Finke 2005, 25). As North (1990) argues, informational constraints exist on two levels. First, the constraints are created by cultural systems of meaning that cause differences in the way information is perceived and interpreted. Second, the constraints are a product of the existence of so-called transaction costs.

The concept of transaction costs dates back to Ronald Coase's "The Nature of the Firm" (1937) and builds on the assumption that market information is not free of cost. As new institutional economists argue, actors need to use time and resources to gather information before they enter a transaction. The costs involved in gathering and evaluating market information are called transaction costs (Furubotn and Richter 2005, 47–76). According to North (1992, 4), the existence of transaction costs indicates that markets cannot be understood as efficient in a neoclassical sense because the efficient market hypothesis assumes that all market actors have costless access to all relevant information. If one assumes, however, that information is costly, markets cannot be seen as evolving toward efficient market equilibrium as the outcome of egalitarian processes of supply and demand. The reason is that actors vary in the quantities of resources they have to invest in collecting and evaluating information before entering into transactions. Following from this, Knight (1992; Knight and Sened 1995) points out that the existing market equilibria do not necessarily represent an advantageous outcome to all market actors. Rather, they are a product of rules created by those with the necessary bargaining power. Institutionally speaking, market equilibrium is thus not a result of processes of supply and demand, but an outcome of institutional arrangements that are influenced by ideologies, social conventions, and power asymmetries.

So what can the concepts of new institutional economics tell us about the economic foundations of market forecasting? Unlike neoclassical economics and behavioral economics, the concepts of new institutional economics are almost fully absent in practical textbooks on financial analysis and rarely ever serve as a point of reference for financial analysts in practice. There are two reasons. First, few new institutional economists have applied the concepts to studying financial market processes. There is, for example, no new institutional study of financial analysis that could provide analysts with a reference point. Also, because it addresses exploitative power relations, for example, the concept of bargaining power, new institutional economics is usually considered a much more radical critique of mainstream economics than behavioral economics is. This is why, when discussing market efficiency, today's neoclassical economists usually mention the critique that comes from behavioral economics but conceal the critique that comes from new institutional economics.[6]

This concealment of the new institutional critique is surprising because, to some degree, the concepts of new institutional economics could help to understand financial analysis as a market practice. Financial analysis is based on a number of norms and conventions. For example, the claim made by fundamental analysts that future values can be estimated by considering economic determinants such as company profits, sales, and expenses can be understood as a convention. It could, therefore, be argued that this convention—or institution, to use the new institutional economists' term—is used to increase the analysts' bargaining power, which they can then use to stabilize possible future outcomes. And, even more strikingly, the concept of transaction costs offers a persuasive way of making sense of the activity of financial analysts. By collecting and evaluating information as a service to investors, financial analysts reduce the investors' need to look for and interpret market information themselves.[7]

In terms of market forecasting, however, the concept of transaction costs does not help to legitimize the market practice. The reason is that, even if they have a relatively large amount of information, market actors still face the issue of not knowing *how* information will affect future stock markets. Furthermore, if institutions (such as conventions governing the practice of fundamental analysis) reduce uncertainty in a financial market context, they minimize opportunities for speculation, for speculation is based on the instability of markets. Beckert and Berghoff (2013, 498) therefore argue that, unlike other economic exchanges where institutions stabilize future expectations, "Capitalistic economies [. . .] are characterized by a specific tension between those institutions reducing uncertainty and those institutions creating uncertainty, especially markets." As a result, uncertainty about future developments is always part of the financial market economy (see Beckert 2013, 2016; F. Knight 1921). It follows that, as in neoclassical and behavioral economics, new institutional economics does not offer a theoretical background that could be understood by financial analysts as a justification of their market practice.

Inside Swiss Banking

I remember when, as a fresh-faced undergraduate student, I skipped class to go to Zurich's Paradeplatz to witness a happening that seemed to me to be of considerable political importance. On June 18, 2002, former US lawyer Ed Fagan visited Paradeplatz to publicly announce a lawsuit that he was launching against a number of Swiss banks concerning their former business activities with the South African apartheid regime. Long before Fagan showed up, the square was crowded with people. Some were observers like me, but many others were people who saw Fagan's attack on Swiss banks as an attack on Switzerland as a whole. The crowd, predominantly consisting of older Swiss males, booed and chanted "go home Fagan." Some of them had made banners, others had brought old vegetables to throw at Fagan. Of course, Fagan did not randomly choose Paradeplatz as the place where he would announce his class-action lawsuit. He chose it as the symbolic center of Swiss banking and wanted the lawsuit to be perceived as a general attack on Swiss banking and its banking practices.

Fagan made the right choice. Paradeplatz has been the dominant symbol of Swiss banking since the end of the twentieth century. It is thus no coincidence that the local activists of the 2011 Occupy Movement chose Paradeplatz to protest against the growing inequalities created by speculative finance (see Juris 2012). The headquarters of Switzerland's two major banks, UBS and Credit Suisse, as well as those of many smaller banks, are on Paradeplatz. In the Swiss version of Monopoly, Paradeplatz is the most expensive place to build a (small plastic) house or hotel. The same might apply to the real world. It is estimated that one square meter sold for between US$40,000 and

60,000 in 2011 ("Vorwärts," 2011). The presence of many of the Swiss banks has meant that Paradeplatz has been the subject of many urban legends. Some people of Zurich claim that the world's biggest volume of physical gold is stored beneath the square. In case of financial trouble, Swiss people sometimes jokingly say, you should go and dig a hole in Paradeplatz. Of course, Paradeplatz is not actually built on gold. Switzerland's two major banks do, however, have some of their safes, in which clients can store their physical treasures, at Paradeplatz.

Although Paradeplatz, which is geographically very small, represents the epicenter of financial Zurich, a number of locations of considerable importance also are attached to it. One of them is Bahnhofstrasse, which is Zurich's largest shopping street. It crosses Paradeplatz and is home to the stores of many of the world's best-known and most expensive fashion designers, to the fashion retailers that are increasingly dominating all larger cities, and to many banks. Another one is Zurich's traditional financial center, to the southwest of Paradeplatz. Today, it is home to a diverse mix of large international banks with a small Zurich branch, Swiss private banks, and a variety of other financial institutions, such as hedge funds and private equity firms.

During the day, the district around Paradeplatz is crowded with men and women in suits, escaping their offices for a quick lunch, coffee, or a cigarette. As a result, many small coffee shops and restaurants have opened in this district. A lot of them are open only during the day. Those that stay open in the evening serve beer, wine, spirits, and food for bankers relaxing after work. In general, the atmosphere in these coffee shops and after-work bars is not as raucous as one might imagine. Unlike New York's Wall Street or London's City, Switzerland's banking culture has always been keen on appearing discreet and humble. This is probably the result of a mixture of Zurich's Protestant background (see Weber [1905] 2009) and a desire to embody the virtues usually ascribed to Swiss banking. In terms of the concentration of wealth, a number of status symbols can be detected. If you drink at one of these bars, you will see Ferraris, Lamborghinis, and Porsches passing by every two minutes. Inside the bar, people's wrists give them away. Not all the bankers wear fancy suits, and many of them change clothes in the office before they go out. But the expensive Swiss watches they wear usually identify them as people with very high salaries.

This microcosm of Paradeplatz and its surroundings offers a great opportunity to see and study bankers in Zurich. Zurich's banking sector is by no means limited to this geographical area, though. In fact, many of the bankers of Zurich do not work here at all, but in the outskirts of the city. Switzerland's two major banks employ about forty-five thousand people in Switzerland alone. From a financial point of view, it would be far too costly to accommodate them all in downtown Zurich. Hence, their buildings at Paradeplatz primarily have a symbolic function. They create a sense of financial potency, of authority, of prestige. Inside the Paradeplatz buildings, most of the rooms are set up for client meetings only. Marble floors, large wooden conference tables, and expensive paintings on the wall: Everything is designed to impress clients. Most wealth managers come from offices outside the banking district to meet the clients there. After the meeting, they return to their own offices that are a good deal less elegant than the opulent buildings on Paradeplatz.

A Brief History of Swiss Banking

Zurich's Paradeplatz and the various locations in the outskirts of Zurich depict the magnitude of Swiss banking as an industry that is crucial to global capitalism today. In 2007, some 28 percent of the global financial wealth stored abroad (*offshore*) was located in Switzerland (Straumann 2006, 139; Wetzel, Flück, and Hofstätter 2010, 352; Zucman 2016). Particularly since the start of the financial crisis in 2007, therefore, Swiss banking has been subject to many political debates (especially in the United States, Germany, and France). Moreover, in movies and literature, Swiss banks are often the places where the bad guys store their money (see, for example, *The Spy Who Loved Me*, *The Da Vinci Code*, or *The Wolf of Wall Street*). Some readers might thus think of it as an investors' safe haven, where money is stored discreetly and responsibly. Others might think of it as being famous for its shady market practices, such as money laundering, tax fraud, and tax evasion. Either way, to many people, Swiss banking is a term with particular connotations.

Swiss banking began in the fifteenth century and is directly linked to the inventors of modern banking.[1] At the beginning of the fifteenth century, Italian merchants, mostly located in Florence, Venice, and

Sienna, started to institutionalize the lending and borrowing of money by introducing double-entry bookkeeping, a calculative practice that paved the way for a more systematic kind of banking. Unlike the step-by-step approaches that had characterized earlier practices of lending and borrowing, double-entry bookkeeping allowed merchants to borrow and lend larger sums without depending on a swift return of the money (Carruthers and Espeland 1991; Power 2012; Valdez 2007).

During this period of institutionalization, the Medici, probably the most successful and influential merchant family of the Renaissance, recognized the geopolitical importance of Geneva (an independent diocese at that time) as a link between northern and southern Europe. Thus, in 1425 they founded in Geneva one of the earliest subsidiaries of what would later become the Banco Medici (Bergier 1990, 327). In addition to its geopolitical importance, Geneva also already had a rapidly growing trade fair, the success of which was reinforced by the presence of the Medici and other Florentine merchants (Goldthwaite 2009). The trade fair, where merchants primarily traded luxury textiles, generated considerable wealth for Geneva for many years. In 1462, however, the trade fair was forced to move from independent Geneva to Lyon in France. This change was brought about by Louis XI of France, who was not happy about an independent region prospering so close to his kingdom. Geneva immediately lost its access to wealth, and Lyon replaced it as the center for merchants (Bergier 1990, 297).[2]

In the centuries that followed, Geneva and Zurich—the two financial centers of Switzerland today—played a subordinate role in supranational trading and banking. In the eighteenth and nineteenth centuries, however, historians report a growing number of sources mentioning a relatively large amount of liquid money and a will to lend money at low interest rates in Switzerland (Cassis and Tanner 1992, 294). This wealth, argue Cassis and Tanner, was the product of a flourishing agricultural sector and the rise of tourism in Switzerland. At this time, most of Switzerland's neighboring countries were already in the process of setting up a more institutionalized system of banking that allowed farmers, merchants, and industrial entrepreneurs to borrow money for the larger infrastructural investments they had to make to keep up with the competitive environment that accompanied Europe's industrialization. In Germany and Austria, the establishment of a network of *Sparkassen* (savings banks) was in full swing. In France, the *banques d'épargne* (savings banks) also started to cover the greater demand for loans.

Switzerland's answer to this development was to set up *Kantonalbanken/banques cantonales*. Organized by the cantons, they were publicly owned financial and savings institutions designed to serve the financial needs of canton inhabitants. During the establishment of these savings institutions, however, a number of families in Switzerland already were very successful merchants and industrial entrepreneurs and there was a great deal of Swiss investment activity in large industrial projects abroad. This led to a dual banking system in the nineteenth century: the cantonal banks enabled the working class and small-scale industrialists to save and borrow money, while private banking networks organized trading and managed investments of wealthy families abroad. It seemed to be just a matter of time until someone came up with the idea of monopolizing this dual market (Bergier 1990; Cassis and Tanner 1992).

In the second half of the nineteenth century, a number of what were called universal banks were founded in Switzerland. As Ritzmann (1973) points out, these new big banks were a "strange mixture of commercial banks, holding companies, central banks, and investment trusts" (quoted in Cassis and Tanner 1992, 295). The strategy of these new banks proved to be very successful. They bought up and integrated many of the smaller financial service providers, and their sheer scale enabled them to become more powerful over time. As Cassis and Tanner demonstrate, the dominance of the new universal banks led to a long period of consolidation, accompanied by a rapidly growing number of assets from 1910 onward (see table 1).

After this consolidation process in the early twentieth century, many of the small private Swiss banks still existed. But the process marked a turning point in Swiss banking: It was a move toward a new style of banking in which larger institutions generated a large share of their earnings by providing saving, financing, and investment opportunities. And unlike banking in other countries, where banking sectors experienced a similar consolidation, these larger Swiss institutions began to focus on managing foreign money, rather than concerning themselves with the wealth of Swiss people alone. Guex

Table 1. Changes in the number of banks, bank offices, and total assets, Switzerland, 1910–60

	1910	1920	1930	1940	1950	1960
Banks	449	378	362	335	325	319
Bank offices	—	—	—	1,051	1,311	1,519
Total assets (in billion US$)	7.9	13.5	21.2	17.2	25.8	50.8
Total assets/bank (in million US$)	18	36	60	51	79	159

Source: Cassis and Tanner 1992, 296

(2000) argues that as taxes rose in some of Switzerland's neighboring countries, Swiss banks started to offer discreetly managed foreign money deposits as a new niche strategy around 1900. At the end of the nineteenth century, Swiss banks already were starting to capitalize on a "practice of secrecy" (Guex 2000, 240). In the early twentieth century, Swiss banks then began actively promoting this secrecy to attract capital from abroad and hence began offering foreign clients the option of hiding their money from tax authorities. As Guex (2000, 241) notes, "This propaganda campaign reached such a level of intensity [. . .] that the Swiss minister of economy, fearful of possible retaliatory measures from foreign governments, felt obliged to ask the bankers to lower the pitch of their message."[3]

SWISS BANKING DURING AND AFTER THE WORLD WARS

As table 1 shows, the amount of assets managed in Switzerland dramatically increased between 1910 and 1960. Straumann (2006) identifies two factors that directly contributed to Swiss banks becoming leading institutions in providing financial services during and after the world wars, and four factors that helped to stabilize their success throughout the twentieth century. First, Straumann argues that Switzerland's political neutrality helped to strengthen the country as a banking location. Second, a new legal framework set up in 1934 increased the confidentiality of client data (part of the framework was today's well-known Swiss bank secrecy).

In the long run, Straumann says, the momentum created by these two factors was stabilized by four other factors. First, Switzerland was well connected at an international level, partially because of the country's four official languages and its prominent position in humanitarian activities. Second, Switzerland was not directly involved in the two world wars.[4] Third, the Swiss banking sector proved to be relatively stable before the world wars. Fourth, Switzerland's political regime was dominated by conservative politics with a focus on economic liberty throughout most of the twentieth century.

Thus, argues Straumann, Swiss bank secrecy was only one factor among many that helped Swiss banking to become so successful. Guex (2000), however, claims that the practice of secrecy adopted by Swiss bankers from the late nineteenth century onward was a significant factor in helping Switzerland become the world's leading wealth management center. In the early 1930s, Switzerland decided to draft a banking act in which the practice of secrecy was legally codified as Swiss bank secrecy. The 47th article of the Bundesgesetz über die Banken und Sparkassen (1934), generally referred to as the Swiss Banking Act in English, defined that anyone who discloses a secret that was committed to him or her as a representative of a bank, a Swiss financial regulatory agency, or another financial institution regulated under Swiss law, will be punished by jail or a fine.

Technically, Swiss bank secrecy itself is not as exciting as one might imagine when looking at its public image. Its specialty, however, lies in a small legal detail: the differentiation between *tax fraud* and *tax evasion*. Under Swiss law, tax fraud is defined as the active deception of regulatory authorities (using forged documents, for example), and tax evasion is defined as nonreporting or incomplete reporting of sources of income or bank deposits to tax authorities. In contrast with the case of tax fraud, if tax authorities suspect tax evasion, Swiss banks are not obliged to disclose information protected under Swiss bank secrecy. Authorities thus have to present evidence of tax fraud (such as forged documents) to gain access to information on the financial standing of Swiss bank clients (Bundesgesetz über die Banken und Sparkassen 1934). From 1934 to today, the Swiss government has been highlighting the fact that Swiss bank secrecy aims to protect privacy. The draft of the federal act submitted on February 2, 1934, however, reveals that the Swiss Banking Act was never about privacy alone. It also was an attempt to strategically strengthen Swiss banking by codifying Swiss bank secrecy. The draft evaluates the banking laws of a number of countries and demands the establishment of a Swiss banking law that will help position Swiss banking in an international environment as being safe and discreet (Swiss Federal Council 1934).

During World War II, the image of safe and discreet Swiss banking delivered its first dubious results. As a group of renowned Swiss historians showed in a large historical assessment, Swiss banks benefited significantly from various shady activities. On the one hand, they stored wealth belonging to dispossessed individuals and families that was transferred to Switzerland by the Nazis. On the other, by referring to Swiss bank secrecy, they later refused to give dispossessed families information about wealth belonging to people killed during the Holocaust (see Bonhage, Lussy, and Perrenoud 2001; Francini, Heuss, and Kreis 2001; Perrenoud et al. 2002).[5] In the postwar era, Switzerland continued to benefit from storing illegitimately acquired and untaxed money. And ever since, Swiss bank secrecy has been criticized for its safeguarding of tax evasion. In Switzerland, these political debates are usually initiated and reactivated by public scandals that erupt every few years.[6]

Today, the role of unreported earnings and wealth is still subject to discussion, and Swiss banks are (for obvious reasons) reluctant to disclose information on this particular topic. Cautious banking exponents estimate that 30 to 50 percent of the total amount of money held in Swiss bank accounts on behalf of foreign clients has not been declared to tax authorities (an estimate by Swiss banker Konrad Hummler, as repeatedly reported in Swiss media). In contrast, Helvea, a Geneva-based think tank, calculated that nearly 80 percent of all the foreign assets held in Switzerland have not been declared to tax authorities (inaccessible study, results reproduced in "Woher das Schwarzgeld," 2010). In 2012, the Swiss government announced a *stratégie d'argent propre* (clean money strategy) in an effort to alter Switzerland's banking image and ease political tensions with the European Union and the United States, who blamed Switzerland for its hosting of undeclared money. Currently, it is still impossible to tell whether this new strategy will be a turning point in Swiss banking or whether it is merely a case of lip service to protect traditional Swiss banking practices from hostile attacks from abroad.

I mentioned that Swiss financial activities were primarily based in

Geneva until the twentieth century. To some extent, Basel also was a place where banking flourished. Zurich did have a solid network of banking institutions, but in terms of being acknowledged as a financial center, it was long considered to be number three after Geneva and Basel. This did not change until the twentieth century, and the consensus on Zurich being Switzerland's premier financial center is relatively recent. Today, it seems to be almost self-explanatory, since Switzerland's two largest banks, UBS and Credit Suisse, both have their headquarters and most of their operational staff in Zurich. UBS was founded in 1998 as a merger between the *Union de Banques Suisses* (founded in 1912) and the *Schweizerischer Bankverein* (founded in 1854). Credit Suisse, the smaller of the two giants, was renamed and restructured in 1997 as a formally new bank based on the *Schweizerische Kreditanstalt*, which was originally founded in 1856.

During the late 1980s and early 1990s, Swiss banking experienced a significant shift. Most of its banking institutions were struggling to keep pace with increases in the turnover of their competitors on Wall Street, such as Goldman Sachs, Merrill Lynch, and Morgan Stanley. As a consequence, many Swiss banks changed their strategy and moved toward more aggressive market behavior (Wetzel, Flück, and Hofstätter 2010, 350). At the end of the 1990s and the beginning of the 2000s, this new aggressive strategy created enormous returns. UBS's stock price doubled within ten years (from US$34 per share in 1997 to US$67 per share in 2007) and Credit Suisse's stock tripled in the same period (from US$31 per share in 1997 to US$93 per share in 2007). By the middle of the 2000s, the two banks were among the most important financial institutions in the world. In 2004, UBS was the world's largest bank in terms of assets under management, and Credit Suisse was number 13 (Valdez 2007, 40; see table 2).

SWISS BANKS DURING THE FINANCIAL CRISIS

The successful strategy that Swiss banks pursued in the early 2000s was hardly questioned by the political and financial establishment in Switzerland at the time. First, this was because the Swiss economy as a whole benefited from the success of the banks, which created new jobs and generated tax revenues. Also, many of the banks actively lobbied for their interests in the Swiss parliament. This uncriti-

Table 2. Top twenty world banks, by assets, 2004

Ranking	Bank	Legal domicile	Assets (in billion US$)
1	UBS	Switzerland	1,533
2	Citigroup	USA	1,484
3	Mizuho Financial Group	Japan	1,296
4	HSBC Holdings	UK	1,277
5	Crédit Agricole Groupe	France	1,243
6	BNP Paribas	France	1,233
7	JP Morgan Chase	USA	1,157
8	Deutsche Bank	Germany	1,144
9	Royal Bank of Scotland	UK	1,119
10	Bank of America	USA	1,110
11	Barclays Bank	UK	992
12	Mitsubishi Tokyo Financial Group	Japan	980
13	Credit Suisse	Switzerland	963
14	Sumitomo Mitsui Financial Group	Japan	897
15	ING Bank	Netherlands	839
16	ABN Amro Bank	Netherlands	829
17	Société Générale	France	819
18	Santander Central Hispano	Spain	783
19	HBOS	UK	760
20	Groupe Caisse d'Épargne	France	741

Source: Valdez 2007, 40

cal stance and lack of regulation toward the banks' aggressive strategy was exposed in 2007 when the financial crisis began. UBS, in particular, had invested heavily in the US subprime market[7] and was one of the most enthusiastic engineers and traders of products such as the mortgage-backed securities and collateral debt obligations that later became the well-known toxic assets[8] (Straumann 2010).

The numbers speak volumes. UBS reported a profit of US$11.9 billion for 2006 and reported a loss of US$4.6 billion for 2007 (Wetzel, Flück, and Hofstätter 2010, 347). As Hablützel (2010) explains, the effect of the financial crisis on Switzerland was much bigger than many people assumed it to be. From summer 2007 to spring 2009, the Swiss banking sector as a whole registered a loss of US$75 billion. On the basis of the country's gross domestic product (GDP), this represents a loss of 17.9 percent. In the United States, banking sector losses totaled only 5.4 percent of GDP in the same time period. In Germany it was 2.3 percent. Although Switzerland's heavy financial losses caused only a minor increase in unemployment rates and were to some extent absorbed by the small and medium-sized enterprises that kept performing relatively well, the country still had to take political steps that hardly anyone would have thought were possible or necessary just a few years before.

In the United States, Bank of America, Citigroup, Goldman Sachs, and many other financial services institutions received financial help via the Emergency Economic Stabilization Act of 2008. Also in Switzerland, the central bank and the government had to take measures to bail out Switzerland's largest bank, UBS. On October 16, 2008, UBS was provided with additional capital of US$71 billion. This step was considered necessary because the bank was perceived to be systemically relevant.[9]

ON SWISS BANKERS

Alongside the changes in strategy of many Swiss banks in the second half of the twentieth century and the beginning of the twenty-first century, the social roles of Swiss bankers have changed dramatically.[10] Until the 1960s, Swiss *banquiers* were usually perceived as uncharismatic, secretive, and mousy people. This image lost its validity in 1964, when George Brown, a politician in Britain's Labour party, coined the expression "Gnomes of Zurich" to discredit Swiss bankers' aggressive speculation against the British pound (Tanner 1993, 21). Suddenly, Swiss bankers were perceived not only as secretive and uncharismatic, but also as aggressive and greedy. Some of the bankers quickly acted out this new role themselves. As the historian Bowlby mentions, some Swiss bankers began answering telephone calls from the United Kingdom by saying, "Hello, gnome speaking" ("Why Are Swiss Bankers," 2010).

I mentioned that Swiss banking went through a structural shift in the 1980s and 1990s. The largest Swiss banks, which had been successful in private banking, began to massively expand their investment banking activities. Swiss banks went from wealth management banks to wealth management *and* investment banking houses comparable to Goldman Sachs or Morgan Stanley. This new direction was driven by a number of key Swiss personalities who had learned about investment banking on Wall Street and in London. For this new investment-oriented Swiss banking, the accountant-like *banquier*, who was still an aspect of the gnome personality, was no longer of any practical use.

This change gave rise to a new type of Swiss banker—outgoing and risk taking—who appeared to represent a more successful way of achieving the financial gains that Swiss banks so desperately hoped to achieve. The framing of this new image of the Swiss banker (replacing the Swiss *banquier*) was inspired by the image and self-representation of Wall Street bankers, who, during the 1980s and 1990s, very much resembled the fictional character of Gordon Gekko in Oliver Stone's movie *Wall Street*.[11] The image's arrival in Switzerland was heavily supported by a number of people of Swiss origin who had experienced the British and US world of finance. Marcel Ospel, who became CEO of UBS after the merger between the *Union de Banques Suisses* and the *Schweizerischer Bankverein*, spent most of the 1980s in London and New York. In a portrait by Claude Baumann (2006, 57; my translation), Ospel talks about "the Protestant culture [. . .] of discipline, achievement, and humility" that dominated his family and his childhood. Unlike many of the former Swiss *banquiers*, Ospel was not a descendent of a wealthy Swiss family. Growing up in a working-class family in Basel, Ospel had to rely on discipline and risk taking, rather than on the family ties or military-based networks that enabled many of his peers to become successful in banking.

Having been socialized into a much more aggressive way of doing business and managing people in London and New York, Ospel's style of managing people fueled a dominant strategy of expansion during the 1990s and early 2000s. When overseeing the takeover of S. G. Warburg by the *Schweizerischer Bankverein* in 1995, Ospel announced that he was going to cut a thousand jobs on the very first day. The British press called it a bloodbath, but Ospel's aggressive and ruthless management style served as a role model for a new generation of Swiss managers who focused on individual performance and risk taking, rather than on traditional Swiss networks (Baumann 2006, 61).

In sociological terms, this shift from relying on traditional networks to adopting a meritocratic system reflects some of the broader shifts in society around that time. Until the 1980s, Swiss banking as a field of work was closely bound to its national boundaries, and bankers were predominantly recruited in Switzerland. As a result, traditional networks, such as the military,[12] the Zurich-based guilds (*Zünfte*), political party affiliations, and networks of influential families were essential in defining whether a person could become a banker. In the late 1980s and early 1990s, these traditional networks became weaker and were eventually almost fully replaced by a meritocratic system. In this new meritocracy, people who wanted to become successful in banking did not necessarily have to be members of traditional networks, but instead had to study at specific universities. (See chapter 4 in this volume for details on Swiss Bank's recruitment process for financial analysts.)

To some degree, this shift in banking had to do with two broader transformations. First, globalization meant that, if they wanted to be successful, Swiss banks could no longer exclusively recruit their bankers and managers in Switzerland. This weakened the significance of Swiss traditional networks. Second, emerging neoliberal ethics in Foucault's (2008) terms, stressed the role of individual merit and thus allowed people who were not part of traditional networks but performed well in competitive environments to enter the field of banking. Ospel, who did not come from a wealthy family but had demonstrated achievements on Wall Street, benefited from both these shifts.

In addition to Ospel, managers such as Lukas Mühlemann (CEO of Credit Suisse, 1996–2000), Mathis Cabiallavetta (chairman of UBS in 1998), and Martin Ebner (owner of BZ Bank, the largest UBS shareholder in the late 1990s) were part of this new generation of bankers. Unlike their predecessors, they were willing to take huge risks and adopt a ruthless style of managing people in the search for short-term gains. This new strategy led to massive growth at the two major banks and to a huge increase in the remuneration of their employees. Baumann (2006, 103) notes that during this time, it became normal for a thirty-year-old Swiss banker to earn a monthly salary of US$15,000, followed by a six-digit bonus at the end of the year.

The transformation of the image of Swiss bankers from being secretive accountants to aggressive and outgoing businessmen and women seemed to be a successful and widely accepted strategy for repositioning Swiss banking in the 1990s and early 2000s. This development was also fostered by the rise of what Foucault calls the entrepreneurial self, the personification of flexibility, competition, and economic interests (Bröckling 2016; Foucault 2008). The start of the financial crisis, however, put a damper on this success. Many exponents of the new generation of managers were held responsible for the involvement of Swiss banks in the subprime crisis. For example, the public blamed Ospel for UBS's subprime activities that made the governmental bailout of US$71 billion necessary in 2008. This failure of the new strategy in Swiss banking called the new social role of aggressive Swiss bankers into question.

Categories of Swiss Bankers

Bankers are often perceived as a homogeneous group. Of course, this perception is legitimate: They all work in banks, they dress in a rather homogeneous way, and they seem to share a considerable number unifying characteristics. From a banker's point of view, however, "the banker" does not exist. The financial analysts I worked with, for example, never referred to themselves as bankers, and they got upset when somebody else did. As I learned in the field, the term *banker* is almost never used as a category of self-ascription.

Bankers themselves put a great deal of effort into differentiating themselves from each other via cultural codes such as clothing, language, appearance, and self-ascription. Using such codes, they try to stress their membership in a professional subcategory in banking, such as trader, wealth manager, or analyst. In the Swiss movie *Snow White*, which was released in 2005, there is a scene that illustrates this attempt to draw boundaries between the various professional subgroups in banking. In the scene, two male bankers meet with two call girls in Zurich's Grand Hotel Dolder. During the conversation, one banker turns to the other and says, "Come on, Brandi, [. . .] tell the girls something exciting about your life in the fast lane. Otherwise, they'll get the feeling that you're a banker, not a financial consultant" (Samir 2005; my translation).

During my fieldwork, I found that distinct professional subcategories could be identified among bankers. These subgroups define themselves by their areas of operation within financial markets. A first distinction that is usually drawn by financial market participants is the difference between people employed in private banking and people employed in investment banking.

Private banking traditionally covers services to private (individual) clients. In terms of activities, private banking is similar to what is known as commercial banking in some countries. In Switzerland, however, the designation "private banking" is usually used to label the services provided to clients with more than US$1 million in their bank accounts. Unlike commercial banking clients, private banking clients are offered more services and are assisted by personal client advisers (a specialized subcategory of wealth managers). Private and commercial banking clients can approach the bank either as lenders, borrowers, or investors. If they lend money to the bank, as is the case with holders of savings accounts, they earn interest for this service. The bank, collecting the money of its lenders, can then lend this money to other clients. Loans are usually given when a client approaches the bank to request a financial credit or a mortgage. For the service of borrowing money, the bank charges its clients interest. Also, private banking clients can act as investors in the market. Here, the private bank offers to process and manage clients' investments for a fee.

Investment banks, on the other hand, do not directly engage with private lenders, borrowers, and investors. Instead, they offer financial services to other corporations. These services include structuring investment products (for example, funds and bonds) or financing large-scale projects for other companies. Investment banks help companies that want to become incorporated and support them in organizing their initial public offering. Also, they are active in mergers and acquisitions, the taking over, restructuring, or liquidation of part of a company or even the entire company.

These different fields of activity for private and investment banks become apparent in the different social roles of their employees. In private banking, trustworthiness and the ability to talk to individual clients are perceived to be of crucial importance. In investment banking, employees deal with more capital and more risk. Their work is usually project-based, and so they have to be able to work under a lot of stress, especially when project deadlines are approaching.

When private bankers and investment bankers talk about each other, many of them reinforce a number of characteristics that are rooted in the differences between the occupations. Private bankers usually describe investment bankers as outgoing, risky, loud, and rude and point to the fact that they do not need to talk to private clients as they themselves do. During my fieldwork, there was one intern who chose to switch from Swiss Bank's private banking department to an investment banking department. This switch was accompanied by a discussion among the private bankers that warned him about the investment banking culture and its perils. "In investment banking," one senior analyst told the intern, "you will be under a lot of stress and your coworkers will be loud and rude." When, months later, the intern visited the former private banking department, he confirmed the warning. He also, however, made it clear that he was proud to be part of this new group now and that he has managed to cope with this rough working environment in investment banking. In a private conversation, he then told me how much he in fact prefers investment banking to private banking. Building on stereotypes that are cultivated among investment banker to describe private bankers, he told me that he is happy to have left the "boring and routinized" environment of private banking.

The categories of private bankers and investment bankers are the most general categories for differentiating bankers in Zurich. These categories, though, are again no more than a very broad bundle of the professional subgroups in banking. In private banking, which is the broad category to which the financial analysts I worked with belong, I could roughly identify five professional subcategories: the employees of the legal and compliance department, the wealth managers and salespeople, the back-office employees, the traders, and the financial analysts.[13]

The *employees of the legal and compliance departments* usually have a background in law and look at banking practices from a legal and risk perspective. In anthropology, their world has been explored in the work of Riles (2004, 2010, 2011), who studied lawyers and regulators as well as legal and compliance employees in finance. Employees of the legal and compliance departments supervise other bankers' activities and normally have an antagonistic relationship with the other groups. Many traders and wealth managers in particular think of the employees of the legal and compliance department as party poopers. In summer 2011, when returning from a meeting at Paradeplatz, I talked to one particular wealth manager about new regulations on client relationships at Swiss Bank. He made it very clear that he was not a fan of the new obligations to check for clients' backgrounds and advise clients on risk attached to trades. "They forbid everything that is fun," he jokingly told me, referring to the members of the legal and compliance department.

Because of their function as guarantors of the legality of business activities, legal and compliance employees usually sit in rooms that are strictly separated from other bankers. They therefore rarely interact with the other subgroups apart from formalized interaction processes, such as exchanging data, reviewing banking practices, and establishing new rules and codes of conduct. As I found out in a number of talks with employees of the legal and compliance department, they prefer to see themselves as being outside the market (rather than being a part of it) and as supervising the activities of the bankers.

The *wealth managers* and *salespeople* are usually referred to as "the front" among bankers. They are the ones who are directly involved in acquiring new clients (so-called prospects) for the bank and in maintaining existing client relationships. In the social studies of finance, they have been explored by Harrington (2016) and, to some degree, by Lépinay (2011). Much of their daily activity is not done at their desks, but during meetings, lunches, dinners, and events where they meet their clients. The wealthier the client is, the more effort the wealth manager can invest in establishing and maintaining the relationship. These efforts often involve traveling abroad and spending whole days or even weekends with the clients. To represent the bank as being prestigious and trustworthy, the physical appearance of the wealth managers is of great importance. Male wealth managers, for example, thus usually wear expensive suits, ties, and cufflinks. This has led to the notion of wealth managers as being snobby and slick, which is an image that is often mentioned by other bankers when talking about wealth managers.

In contrast to the people at the front, the *back-office employees* primarily process the deals that other bankers have closed. In anthropology, Ho (2005, 2009) dedicated large parts of her Wall Street ethnography to this particular professional subcategory. Their work consists of tasks such as managing trade and client information, processing pending trades, and bookkeeping. Even though the back-office employees are the largest group of bankers, they do not see themselves as a prototype of bankers. In the field, I had the opportunity to get to know a number of back-office employees and talk to them about their perception of the other professional subcategories in banking. Many of them described their interaction with non-back-office employees as very reserved and rather uncomfortable. On the one hand, they complained about not being accepted as real bankers by traders, analysts, jurists, and wealth managers. On the other, some of them also stressed that they do not really want to be bankers at all, but just benefit from a well-paid administrative job.

Back-office employees do get relatively high salaries, as well as bonuses. Nevertheless, their compensation is much lower than that of other bankers. Back-office employees thus often have an ambivalent attitude toward the other subgroups. They think of them as overpaid, arrogant, and paternalistic, but many want to become a member of another subgroup one day in order to increase their salaries and bonus and become more influential.

Although trading is mostly done via computers today, it is still a very physical activity. *Traders* are under stress, and they need to take high risks if they want to make profits. Among anthropologists and sociologists who focus on market cultures, traders are the professional subcategory that has been studied most frequently. The very first ethnographies of finance, *Making Markets* by Abolafia (1996) and *The Trading Crowd* by Hertz (1998), both focused on traders. Later, scholars such as Miyazaki (2003, 2013) and Zaloom (2003, 2006) conducted ethnographic explorations of the world of trading. Similarly, much of the work done by financial sociologists has addressed questions linked to trading. Scholars such as MacKenzie (2006; MacKenzie, Beunza, Millo, and Pardo-Guerra 2012; MacKenzie and Millo 2003), Muniesa (2008, 2011), and Stark and Beunza (2009) all studied issues related to technologies and approaches used in trading rooms. In comparison with the other categories, the literature on traders and people involved with trading is thus relatively rich.

In terms of appearance, traders differ from other bankers in many ways. Traders do not dress conservatively at all. They often wear colored shirts. One identifying feature is a colored shirt with a white collar (the Winchester collar). These shirts were sometimes even called trader shirts by other financial market participants in Zurich, because many traders wore them and they rarely appeared on members of other professional subcategories. In the department I spent most of my time, there was one trader whose role it was to link the financial analysis department to the trading floor of Swiss Bank. To exhibit his particular affiliation to traders, he often wore a shirt with a Winchester collar.

Traders also set themselves apart by the way they speak. Their use of language differs radically from the language used by analysts, jurists, wealth managers, and the people from the back office. Often, traders speak about the market in gambling terms, using expressions such as "playing the market" and "betting on a stock." Also, they are known to use very vulgar language, even during their regular work. As Zaloom (2006, 88–89) depicts the setting in her study, traders, for example, sometimes used of the word *cunt* to describe the market. This is a word that, in my experience, never appeared in discussions among other professional subcategories.

Finally, *financial analysts* are highly educated bankers who see themselves as experts on financial markets. As experts, they like to think of themselves not as participants in financial market activities but as neutral observers who identify market trends. The expert status of financial analysts often is reinforced in the way they dress, act, and talk to other market participants. They usually dress in a conservative manner, wearing black or gray suits with no accessories such as cufflinks or colored features.[14]

Such dress codes are normally not articulated, unless a member of the professional subcategory does not adhere to it. This situation arose when David, a young trainee, joined the financial analysis department. David came to work wearing cufflinks and a designer suit. In the first week, the other analysts kept quiet. In the second week, however, David's way of dressing became the subject of discussion among senior analysts. At lunchtime, they asked each other why he had chosen to join the financial analysis department "since he prefers to dress like a wealth manager."

In terms of language use, analysts use wording inspired by economic concepts to signal their intellectual superiority. Their self-perception as a superior group also becomes apparent when they are asked for their opinion of other professional categories in banking. Financial analysts like to portray traders and wealth managers as unintellectual and sometimes even instinct-driven. In anthropology, this book is a first full-scale ethnographic account of financial analysts. Analysts, however, are not an entirely new subject of study for sociologists. Interview material and ethnographic observations of currency analysts working in trading rooms can be found in the work of Knorr Cetina (2011) and Wansleben (2013a). Using interviews, document analysis and historical sources, Beunza and Garud (2007) and Preda (2002, 2007) also studied financial analysts from a sociological perspective.

The categorization of the professional subcategories in banking could of course be broken down even further. In addition to the categories described, the employees responsible for public relations, communication, or technological infrastructure also form subgroups of people who aim to differentiate themselves from other bankers. The great efforts undertaken by members of the various categories to differentiate themselves from each other can partly be understood as a reaction to the strong call for conformity by their employers. Here, items such as cufflinks, Winchester collars, and language use become important ways of stressing individuality. Also, the change in the public's opinion of bankers since the financial crisis has certainly strengthened their desire to avoid simply being identified as bankers.

On an analytical level, the efforts that bankers invest in developing and performing such small professional subcodes are important for two reasons. First, it helps to understand banking and finance as a much more diverse field than is usually perceived by outsiders and researchers alike. Although existing ethnographic research in the social studies of finance never examines financial market participants as a whole but looks at specific professional subcategories, few studies have focused on the processes of differentiation among bankers. To stress this processes of differentiation, however, is important, because it highlights the particularity of findings.

Second, bankers' effort to stress membership of a professional subcategory is of interest when thinking about how financial analysts become influential actors within the field of finance. Among financial analysts, differentiation as a separate professional subcategory in banking is an important way of becoming accepted as a group of market experts. By stressing their intellectual superiority and highlighting their expert status through cultural codes, they actively try to become well respected and thus legitimate actors in financial market settings.

· 4 ·

Among Financial Analysts

Swiss Bank has several tens of thousands employed worldwide. About half the employees work in Switzerland and the other half are spread across the globe.[1] Operationally, the bank is divided into three divisions: private banking, investment banking, and asset management. The private banking division of Swiss Bank is responsible for managing individual client wealth. These individual clients are subdivided into the categories high net worth individuals, ultra-high net worth individuals, and retail banking clients, which are standard categories in private banking. High net worth individuals are clients with between US$1 million and US$50 million in their bank accounts. Ultra-high net worth individuals have more than US$50 million in their bank accounts. In the domestic market, Swiss Bank also offers services to retail clients, who have less than US$1 million in their accounts. That said, the main focus of Swiss Bank's private banking are the high net worth individuals and ultra-high net worth individuals from Switzerland and abroad.

The separation of private banking and investment banking at Swiss Bank is especially relevant in the context of my research because, unlike many other banks, Swiss Bank has two independent financial analysis departments. The investment banking division has a *sell-side* financial analysis department, which creates investment reports that are later sold to other banks and corporations. In contrast, the *buy-side* financial analysis department—the department I studied—produces market advice for use by Swiss Bank's own private banking and asset management clients, who are private investors and corporate clients such as insurance companies and pension funds.

Most of Swiss Bank's private banking division is located in its largest peripheral building that hosts approximately seven thousand employees. The building is located about ten to fifteen minutes away from Paradeplatz and can be reached by streetcar or by bus. In Switzerland, many employees come to work by public transport. Thus, in the morning between seven and nine o'clock, and in the evening between five and seven o'clock, thousands of bankers enter the building or leave it to make their way to the next bus or streetcar stop. Apart from these time slots, the area around the building is relatively calm. Only a few other buildings are nearby, and behind Swiss Bank's building lies a thick forest. Some bankers use their lunch break to go for a run in the forest. For most of the day, however, the bankers stay inside the building.

Inside, not much reminds one of the tranquility that usually surrounds the building. An in-house escalator and twelve elevators connect six large floors filled with workstations. The floors are crowded with workers sitting at computers, leaving their working place for coffee or standing in the corridors and chatting over a drink. It is noisy and hectic and the air is filled with smells from the cafeterias that provide not only drinks but also food. In the corridors, one can hear the telephones ringing in the nearby offices. Moreover, television screens, which are installed in some parts of the corridors, broadcast news on the current state of the economy. It all adds up to a relatively complex soundscape that reminded me of a farmer's market when I entered the building for the first time. And, even though no direct exchange of material goods takes place in Swiss Bank's building, it is in fact a space of today's globalized marketplace.

The vertical arrangement of the departments in the building reflects the internal hierarchy of Swiss Bank. The first floor, which is one floor below the main entrance, is home to the information technology (IT) department. Many of the IT workers at Swiss Bank have an Asian background and I always had the impression that the department has been located on the lowest floor to prevent external clients from seeing these atypical Swiss Bank employees. The second floor is the entrance floor and contains many meeting rooms for internal and external meetings. Because the floor can be viewed from outside the building, it is set up almost as luxuriously as the entrance hall at Paradeplatz. The third and fourth floors belong to the back office, the department that processes trades and does accounting for the deals made by wealth managers. Back-office employees at Swiss Bank typically have a vocational qualification in commercial activities or banking (the Swiss *KV* or *Fachhochschule*). This qualification can be likened to a bachelor degree in the United States. Unlike a US bachelor of arts program, however, a large part of the education takes place in the bank, rather than at a university. Because the demand for this type of employee is large in Switzerland, Swiss Bank runs an apprenticeship program that actively contributes to the training of many people in the back office.

The top two floors of the building belong to three of the most prestigious guilds of private banking: the legal and compliance department, the financial analysis department, and the trading department. The traders are on the top floor, but only a few of them can enjoy the stunning views over the city of Zurich. Most of them sit or stand somewhere in the middle of the open-plan trading room, looking at six to eight computer screens that depict market information, price movements, and buy and sell orders (see Zaloom 2003, 2006). Even though they share the same cafeteria, members of these three guilds rarely interact. Some of them know each other from projects that involve persons from different professional subcategories. For the most part, however, the members of one subgroup stay together while having drinks or eating lunch.

On the three floors where the IT and back-office departments are, the furniture is brown and in a 1970s design. On the top floors, where the trading, legal and compliance, and financial analysis departments are, the furniture is a little more contemporary. I was astonished when I entered the bank for the first time. Beyond the opulent entrance, I found dusty open-plan offices with old carpets and outdated office equipment. The bank's policy of passing on profits to shareholders and to the top management means that long-term infrastructural improvements are rare. The spending policy of Swiss Bank thus creates a working environment in which very well paid people work in relatively threadbare conditions.[2]

Figure 1 shows the setup of Swiss Bank as an ethnographic field. The left side illustrates the hierarchical structure. The stock market analysts, who are at the center of my research, are part of the financial analysis department, which is part of Swiss Bank's private bank-

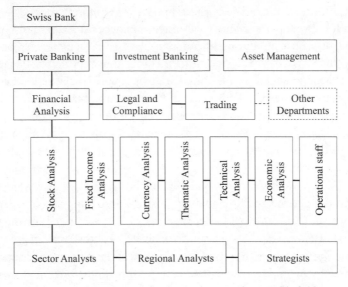

Figure 1. The structure of Swiss Bank as an ethnographic field

ing division. From left to right, I list the other organizational divisions (second row), departments (third row), organizational groups (fourth row), and organizational subgroups (fifth row) that are on the same hierarchical level.

The Financial Analysis Department

The financial analysis department is on the fifth floor, one floor below Swiss Bank's trading floor. The teams of the department sit in two open-plan offices. The operational part of the financial analysis department is in the larger of the two rooms. The operational part consists of roughly thirty IT-support employees who are responsible for putting the financial analysts' forecasts online and twelve editors who are in charge of the printed publications. Swiss Bank uses various formats to publish its analysts' views. They range from short online recommendations and online reports to printed reports and glossy magazines.

Three teams of financial analysts sit next to the operational staff. The largest team is made up of about twenty fixed-income analysts who valuate corporate and sovereign bonds. Valuations of the creditworthiness of companies and countries have long taken a long-term perspective, rather than being driven by short-term changes.[3] Even though this changed during the financial crisis, when government bonds in Eurozone countries such as Greece and Spain became objects of speculation, most fixed-income analysts still stick to their ethos of working in a concentrated, silent, and unemotional way that is fitting for their job of producing long-term valuations. Stock market analysts often say that cooperating with them on topics that involve both stocks and bonds is complicated: "Fixed income analysts don't have any feeling for the market; they don't have to be fast and aggressive," a stock market analyst once told me. On the other hand, fixed-income analysts usually describe stock market analysts in terms similar to those used by stock market analysts when describing traders: loud, aggressive, instinct-driven, and nonintellectual.

Next to the fixed-income analysts, there is a smaller team of currency and commodities analysts made up of about ten people, as well as five technical analysts. Technical analysis is a particular way of making sense of financial market movements and, except for the fundamental analysts' approach, is the most important way of doing financial analysis (Preda 2007, 42). Unlike fundamental analysts, technical analysts do not work with market fundamentals, such as numbers on a company's financial standing or macroeconomic data. Nor do they search for cause-and-effect relationships between a company's intrinsic value and market prices. The only information they use to produce their forecasts is the price that is reflected in the market. They try to recognize patterns in the development of market prices. Anthropologist Caitlin Zaloom (2003) has explored their interpretative work and called them chartists, which is a common term to refer to technical analysts.

The history of technical analysis dates back to the end of the nineteenth century, when ticker tapes first enabled traders and investors to see stock price movements as sequences of numbers. Ticker tapes, which were in use from the 1870s to the 1970s, were paper strips on which were printed the changing prices at which stocks were traded in the market. Soon, the first technical analysts started trying to recognize patterns in these price movements, hoping to find regularities that might indicate how prices would develop in future. Technical innovations that enabled investors and traders to see price movements as curves on computer screens meant that technical analysis became even more popular after the 1970s. Today it is used by many investors and traders as an alternative or supplement to fundamental analysis (Preda 2007, 2009).

In the financial analysis department of Swiss Bank, as well as in most of the other financial analysis departments I got to know during my research, many more analysts engage in fundamental analysis than in technical analysis. As Zaloom (2003) and Wansleben (2013a) illustrated, however, financial analysts located on the floor, that is, among traders, frequently use methods of technical analysis to derive their forecasts. At Swiss Bank, technical analysis received a relatively high level of attention for their numbers: only five analysts did technical analysis, while more than sixty analysts produced their forecasts using fundamental analysis.

What is interesting is that even though fundamental and technical analysts use different styles to come up with predictions, they usually are interested in exchanging market views and engage in discussions. In the second month of my tenure at Swiss Bank, I participated in a training course that had been set up to help new fundamental analysts understand technical analysis. Sam, a young analyst from the technical analysis team, started the workshop by saying, "The price is the only thing that is really distinct of the market. The very core of the economy is the price—a simple measurement of supply and demand in financial markets." Sam then explained a selection of visual patterns that technical analysts usually look for when studying the movement of prices. One pattern he mentioned was "head and shoulders," which describes a visual representation of a price that rises first, then falls, then rises higher, then falls again, then rises a little, and in the end falls back down and thus draws a curve that looks like a head on two shoulders. Other visual patterns that Sam explained were the hanging man, the hammer, and the shooting star. They were all attempts to recognize and name visual patterns in order to predict a future price development.

After Sam's talk, a fundamental analyst participating in the workshop asked Sam why these forms occur. Sam answered, "Honestly, I don't know why they occur. Many academic studies say technical analysis doesn't work, but it does! Maybe it has something to do with mass psychology. [. . .] Fundamental analysts always try to tell a story.

But investors need to understand that sometimes there is no story to be told."

Of course, the work of technical analysts builds on narratives just as the work of fundamental analysts does. Their style of narration, however, differs from the narratives constructed by fundamental analysts. Fundamental analysts use financial and macroeconomic data as a basis for their narratives, but technical analysts build on the market price as a single authority and on psychological effects such as fear, excess, or herding to make sense of market movements.

Even though the logic behind fundamental and technical analysis is many times contradictory, it is interesting that in the financial analysis department I studied, they were frequently combined. Marco, for example, a fundamental analyst with a good reputation, often applied a Fibonacci sequence, an approach used in technical analysis, when he made an investment recommendation. The Fibonacci sequence is a sequence of integers that was named after mathematician Leonardo Fibonacci, who recognized it as a sequence that occurs particularly often in nature. As Fibonacci argued, the sequence is, for example, visible in the arrangement of single leaves of flowers or in growth patterns of bee or rabbit populations (Posamentier and Lehmann 2007).

From a fundamental analyst's point of view, there is no reason to believe that this mathematical sequence could possibly influence the movement of a stock price. The technical analysts of Swiss Bank, however, assumed that a market price curve is more likely to change its direction (from increasing to decreasing or vice versa) in a rhythm of the Fibonacci sequence, which starts with 1, 1, 2, 3, 5, 8, 13, 21, 34, 55, 89, and 144. Hence, when technical analysts recognized a stock price that switched from a price increase to a decrease and back within two consecutive days (1, 1) and then again after two days (2), they argued that it would also be likely that the price would change direction again after three (3), then after five (5), and then after eight (8) days and so on. Following this logic, Marco, the fundamental analyst, usually preferred to wait until the price chart passed a "Fibonacci day" before he published his investment recommendation, even though, apart from his consideration of the Fibonacci numbers, his recommendation was based entirely on fundamental analysis.

The teams responsible for fundamental analysis, thematic analysis, and economic analysis sit in the smaller room of the two open-plan offices of the financial analysis department. The thematic analysis team focuses on thematic issues such as socially responsible investing and alternative energy. The economic analysis team is a small team of six people who look at macroeconomic data. In contrast to the other analysts, they are not bound to a specific asset class of financial market products. The disproportionately small number of economic analysts in comparison with the number of asset class analysts (68 people) is characteristic of how financial analysis works. Macroeconomic developments are considered and analyzed, but the emphasis of financial analysis at Swiss Bank is on the valuation of specific stocks, bonds, and financial products.

The stock market analysis team, consisting of twenty-four members, is the largest team in Swiss Bank's analysis department. Their tasks are arranged according to business sectors and geographic regions. The categorization of business sectors used in financial analysis is strongly influenced by the Global Industry Classification Standard (GICS), a standard developed by MSCI and Standard and Poor's (MSCI 2012; see table 3). The use of a standardized sector classification aims to make financial analysis comparable and allows analysts to share their analyses and forecasts. Sharing similar categories and language codes creates a common language for analysts and a very specific framework for examining and interpreting market developments. The categories and codes influence the way market devices are programed, portfolios are structured, and markets are valuated.

In fundamental analysis, the assumption is that, because companies in a given sector share characteristics, the stock prices of those companies will develop in more or less the same way. As a result, stock analysts are often bullish (expecting prices to rise) or bearish (expecting prices to drop) not only on a single stock, but also on a whole business sector. As Zuckerman (1999) shows, these categorizations of stocks are significant not only in terms of the division of labor among analysts, but also in terms of the valuation of single stocks. Analyzing stock market forecasts between 1985 and 1994, Zuckerman illustrated how stocks that cannot be clearly categorized are less likely to be covered by sector analysts and thus are usually traded at an "illegitimate discount." There is a performative element to the story: if most analysts accept the same classificatory scheme and expect the stocks of one sector to move in a similar way, investors who make

Table 3. Categorization of business sectors and industry groups

GICS Sectors	GICS Industry Groups
Energy	Energy
Materials	Materials
Industrials	Capital Goods
	Commercial and Professional Services
	Transportation
Consumer Discretionary	Automobiles and Components
	Consumer Durable and Apparel
	Consumer Services
	Media
	Retailing
Consumer Staples	Food and Staple Retailing
	Food, Beverage, and Tobacco
	Household and Personal Products
Health Care	Health Care Equipment and Services
	Pharmaceuticals, Biotechnology, and Life Sciences
Financials	Banks
	Diversified Financials
	Insurance
	Real Estate
Information Technology	Software and Services
	Technology Hardware and Equipment
	Semiconductors and Semiconductor Equipment
Telecommunication Services	Telecommunication Services
Utilities	Utilities

Source: MSCI 2012

the investment decisions according to the analysts' opinions increase the probability of stocks within a sector actually moving in a similar way.

The standardization of *regional categories* is less specifically formulated than the categories of business sectors. Nevertheless, a certain consensus exists on how regions are categorized by financial analysts. Much like the sectors, regional categories are important in allowing analysts to develop a common language and make comparable forecasts. Some of the regional categories have proved fairly stable over the last few decades, and others have emerged or vanished more recently. As Wansleben (2013b) demonstrates with the emergence of the

BRIC concept (an abbreviation for Brazil, Russia, India, and China), new categories can become dominant if they are successful in helping to construct a coherent narrative for allocating money to certain regional markets.

Regional descriptions that are frequently used in Swiss Bank's analysis department are LATAM (Latin America), APAC (Asia-Pacific), and MENA (Middle East and North Africa). Two additional regional frameworks that became increasingly popular during my fieldwork are BRIC, used to describe non-Western countries with large and fast-growing economies, and PIGS (Portugal, Italy, Greece, Spain), used to describe EU countries that performed poorly during the euro crisis. Although all analysts use these categories as part of their vocabulary, five analysts are specifically designated to produce regional forecasts for LATAM, APAC, and MENA.

To create proximity to the markets they valuate, Samad and Nasim, two analysts responsible for MENA, are based in Dubai. Kim, the analyst responsible for APAC, is based in Singapore. Another four analysts, who are responsible for the bank's equity investment strategy, are based in London. Prior to the financial crisis, Swiss Bank also had a team of ten analysts in New York. Swiss Bank's overseas locations are frequently expanded or scaled back, very much in line with the bank's expectations about the future market development of the region in which they are located. All analysts abroad have direct reporting lines to Zurich and are frequently contacted via telephone, e-mail, and conference calls by the analysts in Zurich (see figure 2 for an illustration of the geographic distribution of Swiss Bank's financial analysts).

During my fieldwork, I spent one month with Samad and Nasim in Dubai. Swiss Bank's office in Dubai is located in one of the characteristic and gigantic buildings in the city's trading center district. Almost every internationally operating bank has at least a small office in this area of Dubai. Swiss Bank, who puts much effort into offering banking services in the Middle East, employs about fifty to one hundred people in Dubai. Most of them are wealth managers, responsible for clients from the whole Arab region. The ambience differs from Swiss Bank's Zurich office, not only in terms of size and outside temperature. The wealth managers are usually rushing from client meeting to client meeting, and these meetings often take place in hotels, restau-

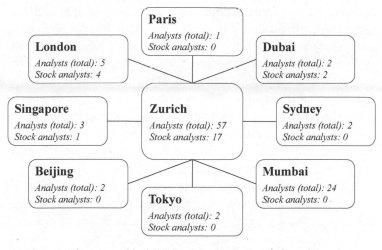

Paris
Analysts (total): 1
Stock analysts: 0

London
Analysts (total): 5
Stock analysts: 4

Dubai
Analysts (total): 2
Stock analysts: 2

Singapore
Analysts (total): 3
Stock analysts: 1

Zurich
Analysts (total): 57
Stock analysts: 17

Sydney
Analysts (total): 2
Stock analysts: 0

Beijing
Analysts (total): 2
Stock analysts: 0

Tokyo
Analysts (total): 2
Stock analysts: 0

Mumbai
Analysts (total): 24
Stock analysts: 0

Figure 2. The geographical distribution of Swiss Bank's financial analysts
(in total and as a share of stock market analysts)

rants, or external meeting rooms. As a consequence, the workstations are often sparsely occupied during the day. The only ones that stayed in the office and from time to time interrupted the monotone noise of the air conditioner were the administrative staff, the people from legal and compliance, and Samad and Nasim.

Samad, whose title is MENA senior equity analyst, is an experienced analyst from London. Nasim, who reports to Samad, is a young analyst from Geneva. As they told me, they both like being in Dubai because of their personal affiliation to the Middle East—both have an Arab background. Also, they told me that they are very well off in terms of salary and living conditions when staying in Dubai. For most of the analysts, working in an overseas location comes with a Swiss contract and a Swiss salary. The deal is even better for those living in a low-tax area like Dubai or Singapore. Also, Swiss Bank pays for Samad's and Nasim's accommodations. In the case of twenty-seven-year-old Nasim, the lodging was a hotel apartment in one of Dubai's hippest hotels, next to the Burj Khalifa.

Swiss Bank also, however, employs analysts overseas for cost-saving purposes. It employs about twenty-five analysts of Indian origin in Mumbai, who provide services to all financial analysis teams in Zurich. Unlike Samad, Nasim, and Kim, the Mumbai-based analysts are hired by an Indian subsidiary of Swiss Bank and earn less than half the salary of an analyst in Switzerland. This cost-saving strategy used by Swiss Bank is referred to as knowledge process outsourcing in management literature (see, for example, Bardhan and Jaffee 2011, 53; Sen and Shiel 2006). In Mumbai, Swiss Bank hires university graduates that are capable of doing financial analysis just as good as the analysts based in Zurich, London, Dubai, or Singapore. The reports they contribute to, however, usually appear under the name of a non-Indian analyst. As Alain, the analyst responsible for Swiss retail companies, once told me, Swiss banking clients would not want to see their investment strategy being produced by an Indian analyst. To avoid accusations of ghostwriting, the reports mention the contribution of an Indian analyst at the end. The front page, however, always features the name of an analyst based in Zurich, London, Dubai, or Singapore.

The typical Swiss Bank financial analyst is male and relatively young, around thirty-five years old. When I first visited the open-plan office, I thought they looked like a very homogeneous group. Of course, the impression also is influenced by the fact that they are all dressed in a similar way: dark suit, white or blue shirt, dark shoes. Everyone is clean-shaven and has short hair—usually styled with hair gel. Some wear a tie, others do not. For the few female analysts, the dress code is not that rigid, but at Swiss Bank they normally adhere to the same basic rules as the male analysts do: no bright colors, few accessories, overall a professional look. In the absence of a tie, they sometimes wear a scarf. Some of the female analysts wear expensive watches, usually a men's model. Talking about her watch, Katrin, a female analyst with many years of work experience in various banks and in various countries, made it clear that wearing a men's watch is one of the few status symbols that allows her to be part of the same symbolic regime as her male peers. Talking to male analysts, Katrin also frequently mentioned her Porsche 911, which was another purchase that allowed her to play in the men's league of status symbols.

Of the twenty-four stock market analysts, only two are women. This ratio more or less represents the overall gender mix in Swiss Bank's financial analysis department. There is also not much diversity of nationality in Swiss Bank's stock market analysis team. Apart from the analysts working abroad, most analysts are of Swiss or German origin, and only two have a migrant background. Moving upward in the hierarchy, this picture changes. Many of the team leaders have a British background. In contrast to the analysts, they are not recruited from Swiss universities but form a part of a globalized banking establishment consisting of expats who change location every few years to get well-paid jobs and powerful positions.

A lot of analysts join the analysis department directly after graduating. After doing the job for a few years, many of them think about moving to another department in the bank. As many of them told me, they expect to earn more money and have more time off "on the front" than they do in the financial analysis department (even though, from my observations, there is reason to doubt that). Their status as experts of the market normally makes them attractive hires for other departments. Hence, with the exception of the team leaders who are pursuing a career within the financial analysis department, most analysts leave the department after five to ten years.

Becoming a Financial Analyst

A number of scholars and journalists interested in financial markets have pointed to the high level of institutionalization in recruitment in finance. In the book *Young Money: Inside the Hidden World of Wall Street's Post-Crash Recruits*, which was published in 2014, investigative journalist Kevin Roose portrays eight young bankers and their experience of joining Wall Street after the climax of the financial crisis. Roose primarily stresses the role that skills play. He starts his book with a list of skills young professionals need to have or must acquire in order to succeed on Wall Street:

> If you want to succeed as a young banker on Wall Street, there are some fairly strict preconditions. You have to be pleasant, polite, and attentive to detail. You have to be able to work three consecutive twenty-hour days without having a nervous break-down or falling asleep on your keyboard. You have to know how to calculate the net present value of future cash flows, how to make small talk about the Yankees, and, ideally, how to write a coherent memo to your boss after your third Jäger bomb. [. . .] But most important, you have to be handy with an Excel spreadsheet. (Roose 2014, ix)

Although Roose's account focuses on the skills that help a person become successful in finance, he overlooks an important factor that decides whether a young professional will even be considered as a potential employee on Wall Street: the educational background. As anthropologist Karen Ho (2009) points out in her book *Liquidated: An Ethnography of Wall Street*, the decision about who gets a chance to work on Wall Street depends heavily on which university a candidate attended. Many Wall Street banks directly recruit candidates from a number of universities, even before they have finished their studies. In her ethnographic account, Ho illustrates how a network between Princeton University and certain Wall Street banks has been established and how, at numerous recruitment events, the importance of this "Princeton family" has been stressed by the representatives of the bank (Ho 2009, 58–66).

In Switzerland, the recruiting of young bankers differs from recruitment on Wall Street as it is described by Roose and Ho. As in Ho's account, however, the university networks that have been replacing military and family networks in Switzerland since the 1980s have become increasingly important during the last decades.

Of the twenty-four stock market analysts that form the team, eighteen are regular employees. Six are trainees who are doing an internship in the analysis department for a short time. For the eighteen regular analysts, a master's degree is the minimum educational requirement. Most of them have graduated from either the University of Zurich or the University of St. Gallen, the two Swiss universities with the best networks to the Swiss banking industry. Unlike those in the global economic analysis team, which is made up primarily of macroeconomists, most stock market analysts studied banking and finance, a very business-driven subdiscipline within economics. Having earned degrees in banking and finance, the new analysts are very familiar with market terminology and some of the approaches used in financial analysis. Swiss Bank actively recruits people who are studying banking and finance at these two universities.

During my fieldwork, I participated in one of Swiss Bank's recruitment events for students at the University of Zurich. For the event, Swiss Bank's management asked two employees to talk about Africa as a continent for future investments. Andy, who at the time covered many companies with exposure to African markets, used his speech to talk about the growing cell phone industry in Africa. Daniel, a wealth manager specializing in socially responsible investing, presented a market outlook for African microfinance institutions. As it turned out during the presentation, Swiss Bank's commitment to African markets and microfinance was not that significant in terms of real investments. Rather, the regional focus was used to present the bank's business as something exciting and exotic that, with its link to social responsibility, goes beyond the realm of economics. Also, by handing out freebies and offering wine and expensive finger food, Swiss Bank cultivated the image of being a place where the students could enter a world of wealth and luxury. At the end of the event, I spoke to some of the students who participated. Some were skeptical about Swiss Bank's presentation, but most were highly enthusiastic about the opportunity to combine the luxurious, the exotic, and the socially meaningful.

During such events, senior analysts and people from Swiss Bank's human resources department actively search for individuals who can be recruited to become financial analysts. In this process, university grades are not of primary importance. Rather, the recruiters look for self-confident, rhetorically strong, competitive students. Marcel, who is responsible for the recruitment process at the University of Zurich, once told me how he identifies a good future analyst. Normally, he explained, he asks the students at the beginning of an event whether someone would like to summarize the event at the end of the day. The students who are willing to do this task become part of Marcel's focus group. Also, if a student actively approaches him or one of the other representatives of Swiss Bank during the event, he or she is more likely to be given the chance to start a career as a financial analyst. As many of these events are for bachelor's degree students, some of the selected students are offered a summer internship.[4] During these internships, students get to know Swiss Bank as an organization and learn how to do some of the basic tasks. In comparison with other internships, they are very well paid, which means they can at least temporarily live the fancy life of a Swiss banker. Usually, the students move to the city of Zurich during this time and become acquainted with urban life.

As an intern at Swiss Bank, students are tested not only on working skills, but also on whether they can adopt the lifestyle of a financial analyst. Marcel, who usually acts as their boss during the internship, makes them work very long hours. Many of them come to the office at about 7:00 a.m. and stay until 6:00 p.m. The reason for the long working days is not that they have so much work to do. Everyone in the department, including the interns, knows that it would be possible to do the daily tasks without doing any overtime. Arriving at the office early and leaving late, however, is a way for them to show that they are highly committed to becoming financial analysts. Marcel usually encourages interns to work overtime as a sign of commitment, and he rewards them for it. In one particular farewell speech that Marcel gave on an intern's last day, he explicitly stressed the intern's ability to work long hours as his primary qualification for becoming a financial analyst one day.

After the summer internship, Marcel usually encourages the students to go back to the university to earn a master's degree. After having accomplished the master's degree, candidates—regardless of whether they interned at Swiss Bank—have to go through an extensive recruitment process. If their initial application is accepted, they first have to be assessed online. The online assessment measures interpersonal, numerical, and linguistic skills. After completion of the online assessment, the selected graduates are invited to a job interview, followed by two additional interviews. The questions posed during these interviews do not follow a standard rule. Newly hired graduates told me that Marcel usually started the first interview by asking them about the gross domestic product of Ghana and a number of other non-European countries. Here again, the focus is not so much on their academic achievements, but on their rhetorical skills, imagination, and self-confidence. Few candidates have any idea about the gross domestic product of Ghana, and so they spontaneously have to come up with an estimation and a story that supports it. Thus, this exercise tests one of the most important skills in financial analysis: the ability to construct a coherent narrative.

Once offered a position at Swiss Bank, senior analysts usually encourage the new members to pursue a chartered financial analyst (CFA) credential. Becoming a CFA involves passing three examinations, each one requiring the memorizing of three to five finance textbooks. Almost all the analysts in the stock market analysis team have at some stage tried to pass the first examination. Because of the high standards, many of them have failed. For the young graduate students, the task is very challenging. They have long working hours, and so they have to study for the examinations on weekends and during their vacation time. If they pass all three examinations, however, the CFA is a strong signal of expertise and distinguishes them from other financial analysts.

In addition to its recruitment efforts at the bachelor's and master's level, Swiss Bank also hires a considerable number of analysts with PhDs. This recruitment is mainly subject-driven. Although junior analysts normally have a background in banking and finance, the analysts with a doctoral degree come from various fields. As a result, the university from which a potential analyst graduated plays a minor role at the PhD level. At the beginning of my fieldwork, I was sitting next to Alex and Sébastien, two analysts who both switched from academia to finance after having completed their PhDs. Both received their PhD from the École Polytechnique Fédérale de Lausanne, Alex in physics and Sébastien in biochemistry. They were hired by Swiss Bank to cover the stocks of companies that are active in the alternative energy and nanotechnology sectors.

As is the case with the CFA, the doctorate creates an aura of expertise. This became apparent when I looked at the situations in which analysts with a PhD mentioned their academic title and at instances where they did not feel that it was worth mentioning. In internal communications and presentations, for example, they rarely ever mentioned it. The reason was that Swiss Bank has no strict hierarchy, and employees usually try to create proximity by using first names and informal language when communicating. Mentioning an academic degree internally would probably be understood as an attempt to create distance. When communicating with wealth managers and external clients, however, analysts with a PhD were very keen on using their academic degree to signal expertise. They added their academic title to investment reports and e-mail signatures and mentioned it in presentations. Even in my case, the managers of the financial analysis department said I should always signal expertise by introducing myself as PhD candidate when communicating on a more formal level.

The importance of educational achievements and degrees that are mentioned on business cards and in personal communication reveals how financial analysts present themselves as qualified experts.

No other department has as many highly educated people as the financial analysis department does. The reason of course is partly the complexity of the analysts' daily work. It is also, however, because analysts, in contrast to other market participants, need to be able to present themselves as the ones who are able to understand the market. When communicating with clients, therefore, they always stress the fact that they have a master's degree, a PhD, or a CFA to underline their symbolic capital, in Bourdieu's (1984) terms, and their ability to understand market movements.

Inside the financial analysis department, educational achievements are no guarantee of success. Former academics, in particular, usually face various hurdles when starting out as financial analysts. First, they have to get used to producing results within a very short time. Timeliness is crucial in financial analysis, and timely analyses are therefore often more important than high-quality research (see chapter 5 in this volume). Furthermore, having spent years in laboratories and at single desks, Alex and Sébastien frequently complained about the noise in the office. A room of fifty other people is obviously never as quiet as a laboratory. Those who held a PhD in economics or political science were less sensitive to the noisy environment, but they also often face a number of difficulties when entering the financial analysis department. Financial analysis is not a straightforward process that can be learned step by step. Beyond calculation and scientific expertise, intuition, storytelling and an authoritative appearance play a significant role. Junior analysts who started at Swiss Bank as interns are well socialized into these processes and systems of meaning. PhD graduates enter at a higher hierarchical level and are directly exposed to competition with analysts who have been in the department for a long time. They have to learn about the calculative and affective sides of financial analysis and find ways to produce meaningful narratives within a very short time. Adhering to the financial analysts' knowledge regime is often a hard and painful experience at the beginning.

Moreover, to become an accepted member of the group, analysts have to go through an initiation on a social level as well. Many social events serve as initiation rites for new analysts to become accepted members of the group. These events are usually linked to going out and drinking beer. Analysts do not necessarily have to drink alcohol in large quantities to become accepted, but if they get drunk with a number of other analysts, the team is likely to accept them sooner. The Christmas season in particular offers plenty of opportunities to go out and drink. In November and December, analysts are invited to Christmas parties, which are usually organized by other banks with business relationships to Swiss Bank. During the two Christmas seasons I spent with the Swiss Bank analysts, many of the newcomers used these opportunities in a strategic way and joined the other analysts at dinners and parties.

Drinking with the other analysts is not an easy task. Some of the experienced analysts try to make the new analysts drink too much and do embarrassing things (such as stealing items in an expensive restaurant or dancing stupidly), and the new analysts always have to be aware that there is a very thin line between what they can do and what they cannot do. Not drinking at all, for example, is not an option for male analysts. Getting drunk too fast and then taking too friendly a tone with the other analysts or being offensive also is perceived badly. Aware of the importance of being fun and outgoing without being embarrassing, new analysts are normally very nervous before these social events. They know the senior analysts sometimes actively seek to make them lose their decency.

One particular Christmas dinner in December 2011 turned into an initiation rite for a number of analysts. At the time, the whole financial analysis department was going through a restructuring phase and William, a British analyst with good reputation, became the superior of many analysts in Zurich. William was known to be a party animal, and so the analysts knew in advance that there would be an implicit requirement to drink a lot during this particular Christmas dinner. To prepare for this task, some of the new analysts organized a lunch in a restaurant. As they communicated it, the reason for this lunch was to eat something rich in calories, which would then prevent them from getting drunk to early. Hence, many chose to eat sausages and mashed potatoes.

When everyone arrived at the restaurant in the evening, William immediately ordered beers for all the male members of his new team. The two women in the team were free to choose what to drink. Katrin decided to have a diet Coke and Jenny ordered a beer. Before finishing half of the first beer, William ordered the next round of beer for all the male analysts. After he repeated this procedure a couple of times, although some members of the group still had full glasses of beer in front of them, people started asking for a time-out. William ignored their request. Tobias, a senior analyst who was not exactly a new member but had to go through this initiation process because of the restructuring of the teams, started to hide his full glasses under the table in order to keep up with William. By this stage, some of the analysts were already struggling to articulate their thoughts. After a few hours of excessive drinking, William started to interrogate the new members about their former bosses. He also came up with a number of stories about each of them and made them look silly.

Later that evening, after the female members and some of the more defensive drinkers had left, William asked the team to join him at another bar. The next day, stories about the dinner were circulating in the office. It was especially interesting to see how the members who had stayed out with William until the very end of the night seemed to manage to establish close bonds with him. The gender dimension also is of particular interest here. Initiation rites in banking often involve the consumption of beer and visits to gentlemen's clubs. Although the male bankers become part of the group by joining the more established group member and behaving in a silly way, the role of female bankers remains undefined. As Zaloom (2006, chapter 5) notes in the context of a traders' Christmas party in Chicago, these initiation rites produce a sphere of masculinity that is very difficult for female bankers to enter.

· 5 ·
Intrinsic Value, Market Value, and the Search for Information

When I started my fieldwork, Marco, who was my mentor at Swiss Bank and introduced me to financial analysis, gave me two textbooks to read. The first one was called *Investments* and was an educational textbook of approximately a thousand pages written by the economists Zvi Bodie, Alex Kane, and Alan J. Marcus (2002). The second book was *Valuation: Measuring and Managing the Value of Companies* and was written by Tom Copeland, Tim Keller, and Jack Murrin (2000). "From now on, they will be your bibles," Marco said, stressing the importance of the textbooks. Indeed, as I learned later, these two textbooks were frequently used by many of the financial analysts. Some analysts had a physical copy of them lying on their desks. Others at least knew where to find them in Swiss Bank's internal library. Those who possessed a physical copy actively used it as a manual to look up working steps or explanations of mathematical formulas.

Textbooks such as *Investments* or *Valuation* are important to financial analysts for two reasons: First, they create a certain degree of legitimacy for fundamental analysis by referring to the shortcomings and theoretical criticisms of the efficient market hypothesis. To fundamental analysts, the conceptualization of intrinsic value is at the core of their work. In contrast to the efficient market hypothesis, practical textbooks used by financial analysts state that the market value as depicted by the stock market price does not necessarily reflect the intrinsic value of a company.

Second, textbooks offer financial analysts an indication for how to come up with market forecasts and how to process and operationalize information while doing so. Financial analysts collect, weight, and interpret information every day. A strong hierarchy of information sources exists, and sources of information are usually judged on their timeliness, applicability, credibility, and originality. Because many sources of information fulfill one or two, but usually not all, of these requirements, the ranking of information sources becomes an important endeavor. Hereby, the treatment of information is never mechanical but embedded in complex processes of interpretation. Here, it is interesting that textbooks acknowledge the fact that the search for information is ambiguous and that forecasts are based on an eclectic combination of calculative approaches, strategies, and interpretative schemes by fundamental analysts.[1]

Fundamental Analysis in Textbooks and "in the Wild"

In 1934 Benjamin Graham, an investment fund manager, and David L. Dodd, an associate professor of finance, published a book that laid the groundwork for fundamental financial analysis. In *Security Analysis: Principles and Techniques*, they called for an analytical approach to looking at financial market movements. At the beginning of the book, the authors make the following statement:

> Analysis connotes the careful study of available facts with the attempt to draw conclusions therefrom based on established principles and sound logic. It is part of the scientific method. But in applying analysis to the field of securities we encounter the serious obstacle that investment is by nature not an exact science. The same is true, however, of law and medicine, for here also both individual skill (art) and chance are important factors in determining success and failure. Nevertheless, in these professions analysis is not only useful but indispensable, so that the same should probably be true in the field of investment and possibly in that of speculation. (Graham and Dodd [1934] 1940, 17)

The eight-hundred-page text that follows this call reads very much like an instruction manual. In laying out a step-by-step approach, however, Graham and Dodd do more than simply establish the idea that financial market movements can be assessed analytically. They also introduce the assumption that corporations have an intrinsic value and that this value can be estimated by an analyst. This intrinsic value, the authors note, "is understood to be that value which is justified by the facts, *e.g.*, the assets, earnings, dividends, definitive prospects, as distinct, let us say, from market quotations established by artificial manipulation or distorted by psychological excesses" (Graham and Dodd [1934] 1940, 20-21; italics in the original). Hence, Graham and Dodd conceptualize the fundamental analyst as a presumably rational actor within an irrational market environment.

The call for an analytical approach that differentiates intrinsic value from market value reads like a counternarrative to the efficient market hypothesis, and it still resonates in the textbooks used by practitioners today. In Bodie et al. (2002), for example, the authors draw a differentiation between market value and intrinsic value and use the differentiation throughout the book. Whenever they explain the analysts' work, the authors use the term *intrinsic value* to describe the outcome of the analysts' estimations. It is interesting that rather than simply ignoring it, the authors devote an entire chapter to the question of market efficiency and criticisms thereof. After having reviewed the neoclassical debate on market efficiency, however, the authors formulate a rather anthropological question: If all the information in an efficient market is taken into account, they ask, what *human practices* lead to the inclusion of market information in stock prices? This question is surprising because neoclassical economic theory rarely mentions the human activity that leads to the construction of so-called efficient markets.[2] Aiming to answer the question of what makes markets efficient, Bodie et al. come to the conclusion that financial analysts are in fact the market participants who integrate information into markets so that their information becomes reflected in the market price.

Analytically speaking, this conclusion points to an intriguing paradox that characterizes the work of financial analysts: By collecting and integrating information into the market, financial analysts make it possible for others to perceive markets as being efficient. This perception, however, means that confined economists (as opposed to economists in the wild—see Callon 2007, 341) see financial analysts as illegitimate actors. Moreover, to ask about the human practices that make markets efficient also points to the fact that Bodie et al. are aware of the economy's reflectivity: The action of financial analysts affects their object of analysis (see Holmes 2014). The awareness of this reflectivity differentiates the textbooks and the analysts' experience from the positivist approach of Chicago-style neoclassical economics.

After reflecting on the efficient market hypothesis, the authors move on to introduce fundamental analysis as the most widespread style of doing financial analysis. They define it as follows:

> Fundamental analysis uses earnings and dividend prospects of the firm, expectations of future interest rates, and risk evaluation of the firm to determine proper stock prices. Ultimately, it represents an attempt to determine the present discounted value of all the payments a stockholder will receive from each share of stock. If that value exceeds the stock price, the fundamental analyst would recommend purchasing the stock. (Bodie et al. 2002, 348)

This definition reveals two things. First, it shows that the determination of the difference between intrinsic value and market value is linked to a number of calculative approaches. Second, it shows that these calculative approaches are always bound to a number of uncertain factors, such as expectations of interest rates and future dividend returns. The existence of uncertain factors means that these calculative approaches can never lead to precise results. Their outcomes are always estimations.

The authors point to the fact that there is not one but many approaches to determining a company's intrinsic value. The most basic approach analysts learn from textbooks is the determination of book value. Book value expresses the current value of a company by comparing its income and expenses. Comparing this book value to the market value, however, reveals an issue: Although the book value gives only an insight into a company's current worth, the market value also reflects investors' expectations about the future development of a company. Here, to calculate these expectations, financial analysts thus have to come up with estimations again.

At Swiss Bank, analysts can come up with their own estimations or consider multiple sources and get estimations from other parties. Some of these estimations, such as future interest rates and overall economic outlooks, are published by national statistical bureaus and university centers. Also, providers of financial market information such as Bloomberg and Reuters publish future outlooks on market developments. And most important, Swiss Bank has its own team of macroeconomic researchers who produce overall market estimations that stock analysts can use for their work. What is interesting is that no rule tells analysts which estimation they should use in their own work. This is because fundamental analysis is not so much about strict calculation as about using numbers in a creative way to support particular investment narratives formulated by financial analysts. In order to look for numbers that are in line with an overall investment narrative, analysts need to have a repertoire of estimations to choose from. Analysts are aware that, much like their own estimations, the market estimations of other parties entail specific interpretations and visions of the future that they may or may not share.

In the meetings I attended, estimations were indeed often subject to debate. After one meeting, Michael, an analyst responsible for stocks in extraction companies, told me that it is crucial for analysts to be free to choose which estimations they use for their analysis. Choosing which numbers to use is part of becoming a good analyst. Michael said that if every analyst used the same estimations, they would all come up with the same future scenario. This, again, would question the role of analysts as experts who produce their own original interpretations and scenarios. Stressing the importance of the freedom to choose which estimations to use, and of the need to come up with original interpretations, reveals a critical point about the work of financial analysts. In the highly unstable and uncertain environment of financial markets, the work of financial analysts creates a *sense of agency* for both the analysts themselves and the investors who have access to the analysts' reports.

Fundamental analysts sometimes rely on external providers for estimations, but they also produce numbers themselves. This is particularly true for the calculative approaches that financial analysts use to come up with a future target price, which is the price at which they feel a stock could be traded at some point in the future. Different analysts choose different approaches to select the various factors that help them to come up with a target price. The textbooks offer a variety of calculative approaches. Some analysts work with the discounted cash flow formula (DCF), whereby a future cash flow is discounted onto the present. Discounting means that payments have a different value that depends on the point in time a payment is received because of the interest attached to the payment. The earlier a payment is received, the more value it has, because the recipient of the payment may use the money to generate interest. As Bodie et al. (2002, 566) state, however, the problem with the DCF formula is that it is based on the assumption that the economy is relatively stable and constantly growing. In the case of a crisis or a period of zero or negative interest, the DCF formula becomes difficult to apply. This is why some analysts prefer to work with other formulas, such as cash flow return on investments (CFROI), return on invested capital (ROIC), and total return to shareholders (TRS). Others, again, focus on ratios such as the earnings per share (EPS), and the price per earnings (P/E) ratio.

Much as in working with estimations from external parties, analysts are keen to avoid having to choose a single calculative approach. Rather, they want to be able to switch between approaches and combine them in a personal way. The exact way in which they use and combine calculative approaches, however, is a well-kept secret. Analysts rarely ever reveal their specific approach when talking with each other. As Michael explained to me, analysts need to find their own way of using calculative approaches to come up with a target price.

It is interesting to note that financial analysis textbooks promote the development of such individualistic styles of valuation. Bodie et al. (2002, 593) state that "if history teaches us anything at all, it is that the market has great variability. Thus, although we can use a variety of methods to derive a best forecast of the expected holding-period return on the market, the uncertainty surrounding that forecast will always be high." As a result, analysts have to look at the various approaches and ratios described in the textbooks and decide which ones they consider to be important and how they want to use them when constructing market forecasts.

Stock market forecasting based on fundamental analysis is a question of imagining a possible future. To do this, analysts have to develop what they refer to as a strategic perspective. By this they mean a narrative that is in line with their calculative approaches and estimations. The finance textbook of Copeland, Koller, and Murrin (2000) explains the importance of constructing this type of strategic perspective. In a chapter on forecasting performance, the authors present a five-step approach to developing a financial forecast:

(1) Determine the length and level of detail for the forecast. We favor a two-stage approach, a detailed forecast in the near term followed by a summary forecast for the longer term. (2) Develop

a strategic perspective on future company performance, considering both the industry characteristics as well as the company's competitive advantages and disadvantages. (3) Translate the strategic perspective into financial forecasts: the income statement, balance sheet, free cash flow, and key value drivers. (4) Develop alternative performance scenarios to the base case you developed in steps 2 and 3. (5) Check the overall forecasts (the resulting ROIC [return on invested capital] and sales and profit growth) for internal consistency in alignment with your strategic perspective. (Copeland et al. 2000, 233)

What is interesting here is that the strategic perspective (step 2) is developed before the quantitative measures (step 3) are considered. It is therefore not the calculation that serves as the basis for the narrative, but the narrative that precedes and frames the calculation (see Latour and Woolgar 1979). During my fieldwork, I made this exact observation over and over again. Numbers do not tell stories; numbers are used to enrich previously constructed stories. When I discussed calculative approaches with stock market analysts, they usually talked about the numbers resulting from DCF, CFROI, and EPS calculations as loose references, rather than hard facts. Analysts use such calculations as an orientation aid. The various signals that are created by these calculations mark the direction that their investment narrative should more or less take.

By differentiating intrinsic value and market value, fundamental analysts create a space in which calculation, interpretation, and anticipation become possible to them. The space produced by this distinction of values also enables analysts to include affective elements and creates the opportunity to frame predictive practices as something individual, which goes beyond the execution of calculative approaches. It thus contributes to the production of the role of financial analysts as experts of financial markets.

The Search for Information

Financial analysts use the figures reported by companies and estimations of macroeconomic development as bases for calculative approaches. Their search for information goes, however, far beyond that. Analysts collect information of all sorts and they strongly believe that any kind of information, independent of whether it is construed as economic in the narrow sense, can eventually affect future market developments. For this reason, the financial analysis department is filled with newspapers, business reports, and market devices that transport information from the outside world to the financial analysis department. The analysts' view of the markets is supported by devices that present information in a ready-to-use format. Four stand-alone Bloomberg stations, as well as a television screen broadcasting Bloomberg TV, are located in the stock market analysts' open-plan office. These devices provide analysts with current stock prices and a wide variety of data on the companies they valuate.

The analysts sit at small single desks, normally in groups of four to six desks, and work on computers with two screens each. In addition to the keyboards and their cell phones, most analysts have stacks of reports, newspapers, magazines, and books on their desk. Of the newspapers lying on the analysts' desks, the *Financial Times* features the most frequently. Its pale salmon color is part of the visual landscape of the department. The stock market analysis teams have about six subscriptions to the *Financial Times*. Usually, the team leaders skim through it in the morning and pass on articles of interest to the analysts who cover a specific topic or sector. Occasionally, you also see Swiss newspapers such as the *NZZ*, the *Agefi*, and *Finanz und Wirtschaft*, as well as the weekly magazine the *Economist*.

In addition to newspapers, weekly magazines, and business reports, a considerable number of books are stored in the open-plan office. These books are either financial analysis textbooks or books about economic, political, and social trends. An enormous amount of information also is kept on the individual companies they cover: annual reports, corporate social responsibility reports, and advertisements sent to the analysts by the companies themselves. In addition to the newspapers, reports, and books, such promotional items are part of the landscape of many of the analysts' desks. A positive valuation by the financial analysts is very important to the companies being valuated. They therefore provide analysts with business information, as well as small gifts, such as toy cars from automobile manufacturers or photo calendars from retail brands. Through these gifts, companies try to establish a personal connection with the analysts. Swiss Bank, however, has strict regulations in place to prevent companies from influencing its analysts' opinions. There are, for example, strict rules on how valuable a gift given to an analyst can be.

Still, personal networks are an important source of information to any analyst. Access to unconventional information helps to strengthen an individual investment narrative, which is why analysts have piles of business cards on their desks. Such business cards are often fetishized. In the movie *American Psycho*, this fetishism is nicely illustrated in a scene in which Patrick Bateman, played by Christian Bale, compares his business card to the business cards of four of his colleagues. Discussing the color, the font, and the quality of paper of everyone's business card, they reveal that business cards are much more than just small printed cards, but symbols of a person's position in business and of his or her taste. The fetishizing of business cards was even more striking during my time of research because, in contrast with 1991 when the original novel *American Psycho* was published, contact details can now easily be looked up online or exchanged via e-mail.

The business cards that analysts collect contain e-mail addresses and telephone numbers of sell-side analysts, external think thanks, company representatives, and people from academia. The number of business cards stored by an analyst represents the scale of the analyst's network. It is important, however, that these contacts are not just a collection but could theoretically be of value to the daily tasks of the analyst. The ability to use the business cards to get valuable information was occasionally tested by other analysts. Sometimes they looked at the business cards of other analysts and asked them for more details about the person mentioned on a card. If an analyst revealed that his or her business cards were merely a sign of prestige and could not really be transformed into a network of informational exchange, the other analysts would think of him or her as a collector of useless cards rather than as a holder of a prestigious collection of cards that represents a valuable network.

Networks are one among the basic foundations of all markets. Apart from that, economists and anthropologists have both claimed that markets, from small-scale bazaars to global capital markets, are organized around information. As Geertz (1978, 30) notes, "the search for information—laborious, uncertain, complex, and irregular—is the central experience of life in the bazaar." Similarly, scholars in the field of the social studies of finance have stressed the role of information in globalized markets. As Stark and Beunza (2009, 118) state, however, collecting information is never simply a matter of quantity, but a matter of selecting the information that is considered relevant to the study of market movements. They refer to this selection process as the cognitive ecology in which market participants operate. In this cognitive ecology, the selection and interpretation of information is more important than the simple collection of information.

The focus on the selection and interpretation of information, as highlighted by Stark and Beunza, calls the efficient market hypothesis into question. As Stark and Beunza show, *even if* the same information is available to all market participants at the same time, the existence of a cognitive ecology still indicates that different market actors will use information sources in different ways and thus will not arrive at the same conclusion about how particular pieces of information might affect the market.

As a part of drawing their conclusions, analysts treat numerous information sources in very different ways. Some sources provide information that can easily be applied to stock market forecasting, and others are considered highly credible but not very timely. Because of these differences, the information that is collected is always *ranked* in a specific way, even though analysts never make the ranking explicit. In order to be of value to financial analysts, information must either be timely, applicable, credible, or original (see table 4).

TIMELINESS

In financial analysis, the timeliness of information is an important feature. Analysts assume that, after a certain amount of time, public information becomes priced in, that is, reflected in the stock price of a specific equity share. This way of thinking about information corresponds to the assumption of the efficient market hypothesis. Analysts think, however, that after information becomes publicly available, they have a considerable amount of time in which they can interpret the information (which is an assumption most confined economists would reject). Financial analysts thus think that they can be faster than the market. As Lépinay and Hertz (2005, 272) put it, they consider themselves to be the gatekeepers of market efficiency. It is only *after* their engagement with published information that markets become efficient.

Table 4. Ranking of informational sources

	Timeliness	Applicability	Credibility	Originality
Academic journals	Slow	Very low	Very high	High
Academic literature	Very slow	Very low	Very high	High
Bloomberg financial data	Very fast	Neutral	Neutral	Low
Bloomberg news data	Very fast	Neutral	High	Low
Broker reports	Fast	Very high	High	High
Company websites	Very fast	Neutral	High	Very low
Company statements	Neutral	Neutral	Very high	Very low
Newspapers	Fast	Low	Low	Low
Online news services and blogs	Very fast	Low	Very low	High
Other analysts	Fast	Very high	Neutral	Neutral
Special-interest magazines (e.g., the *Economist*)	Neutral	Neutral	High	Neutral
Special-interest newspapers (e.g., the *Financial Times*)	Fast	High	High	Neutral

Once financial analysts have processed the information and a particular interpretation has become dominant among financial market participants, the information is considered to be reflected in the price, and the information no longer has any value for the analysts. As Knorr Cetina (2010) notes, the value of information in financial markets is therefore radically different from the value of information in areas such as science: Scientific information (and knowledge) stabilizes over time, information in financial markets loses its value over time. As Knorr Cetina (2010, 176) argues, "Information knowledge," as found in financial markets, "has a time index: it loses its clout after a period of time and then is no longer considered informative."

The fact that information in financial markets has a time index urges financial analysts to act promptly. At Swiss Bank, the financial analysts gathered each Monday and Friday to discuss current market movements and to talk about information on events or trends that they felt were not yet reflected in stock market prices. For the Monday meeting, the analysts often brought along news articles and presented ideas they came across over the weekend. While I was with Swiss Bank, these meetings often resulted in discussions about whether such news and ideas were already reflected in the market price. David, a young trainee who had just finished his bachelor's program and was spending a year at Swiss Bank before starting his master's program, often brought articles from the *Economist* to the Monday meetings and talked about an event, trend, or idea mentioned in the article and its possible effect on the markets. In many cases, the senior analysts listened to David and highlighted the importance of the event, trend, or idea he had presented. After a while, however, one senior analyst usually brought up the question of whether the piece of information brought forward by David was not already reflected in the market price. At this point in one meeting, Marco, the team leader, said, "Basically, we should not look at the *Economist*. Once something is in the *Economist*, it is surely already in the price. We need to look at blogs and online news services. These are the places where we'll find unpriced information—not in the *Economist*."

Analysts spend a lot of time searching for information they consider to be unpriced. Outside the reporting season, which is when every analyst knows in advance what day a company will publish its quarterly results, the search for unpriced information plays a central role. Often, unpriced information becomes available after an event that is expected to influence stock prices. These events can be economic events, but they also are often of an environmental, political, or social nature. Unlike economic events, environmental, political, and social events are usually less anticipated by analysts. When such events occur, however, they can have a big effect on the stock market. If a major event of any kind occurs, analysts first discuss what effect the particular event might have on stock market development. Generally, they argue that any kind of event affects the market in some way.

The Fukushima nuclear catastrophe and the numerous events connected to the Arab Spring were among the most important unpriced events I encountered during fieldwork (see Leins 2011). When such events occurred, the financial analysis department was in a state of emergency. From one moment to another, the mood in the open-plan office became hectic, telephones started to ring, and analysts were sprinting from their workstations to the next Bloomberg station and back, trying to get a picture of what was happening and how it affected the market. No matter how poor the available information was and how embryonic a first interpretation of the event looked, such unpriced events forced financial analysts to come up with a reaction, and possibly new investment advice, within twenty-four to forty-eight hours. The investment advice was usually meant to help the bank's clients either protect themselves from falling stock prices or benefit from rising ones. Also, these reactions reinforced the idea that financial analysts can quickly amend investment strategies when presented with new information.

On these eventful days, news commentators and journalists stressed the greater uncertainty linked to Arab Spring or Fukushima, but analysts and investors do not necessarily see such events as purely threatening. Destabilizing events also present financial opportunities. Markets offer speculative instruments that can leverage financial benefit from events regardless of whether the effect is positive or negative. In the case of an event that is expected to have a negative effect on a stock price, investors can, for example, short-sell the stock before its price drops. Short selling is an investment strategy that is never actively recommended by Swiss Bank's financial analysts. It is, however, often recommended by wealth managers. In short selling, investors sell a stock they do *not* hold in their portfolio, which gives the investors the opportunity to buy the stock at a lower price after a while and compensate for their short position. If the scenario of a decreasing stock price materializes, the investor gains money from the drop in price.

In the case of events such as the Arab Spring and Fukushima, financial analysts are thus not primarily interested in the nature of the event, but in the appearance of unpriced information surrounding the event. In such a case, financial analysts have to act fast to make sure that their investment advice reaches the client before the information is priced in. Many analysts claim that information is too old to use for speculative purposes as soon as it is published in mainstream (financial) media. This perception influences the use of information sources during such events. Many analysts prefer to use blogs or online news streams that promise prompt and potentially unpriced information. Of course, such information sources also have shortcomings. First, analysts have to deal with the fact that they do not know how reliable the information is. Second, the information entails no interpretation about how it might affect markets.

One problem analysts face when working with prompt information is that, in order to have an effect on stock markets, the information must be identified as a potential market mover not only by them but also by other financial market participants. If only one financial analyst thinks a particular piece of information is significant to the markets, it is unlikely that the information will ever be reflected in the market prices. Keynes (1936) famously explained this phenomenon by comparing stock market valuations to a newspaper contest that asks its readers to guess the future winner of a beauty contest from pictures. Here, it is not important which participant a reader considers to be the most beautiful. Instead, readers have to work out which participant might be perceived as the most beautiful by the majority of other readers. To produce lucrative predictions, analysts must likewise anticipate the opinion of the other market participants. In other words, in developing investment strategies, analysts cannot simply look for information they consider to be relevant; they have to look for information they think other market participants also will perceive as relevant. Analysts thus become second-order observers (Luhmann 2000; Stäheli 2010, 358). They include the observations of other observers into their practice in order to develop their stock market forecasts.[3]

The importance of gathering timely information not only manifests itself in the search for information at times of events. It also structures the daily schedule of financial analysts in general. At Swiss Bank, the analysts normally arrive at the office between 6:45 a.m. and 7:30 a.m. At that time, the senior analysts, who are responsible for identifying and interpreting market trends, have already checked their mobile devices for timely information on their way to the office. Once at the office, they start to search for online information sources and read incoming reports from sell-side analysts, who usually start work even earlier. On calm days (when no out-of-the-ordinary events influence markets), analysts spend their time reading newspapers and surfing the Internet. At this time in the morning, Asian stock markets are already open, but the financial analysts normally find time to read and gather information and to organize their daily tasks until the Swiss stock exchange opens at 9:00 a.m.

Throughout the day, the importance of gathering timely information is omnipresent. In meetings and during their lunch breaks, analysts usually use their mobile devices to stay updated about the latest market developments. Swiss Bank's cafeteria on the top floor, where the traders and the analysts get their coffee, has three television screens that broadcast news from the financial world. During coffee breaks, analysts usually have one eye on these screens and discuss possible interpretations of the news and market developments with the other analysts on the break. To many analysts, the search for timely information becomes an obsession that is not limited to the hours they spend in the office. Analysts also frequently communicate new information from home during the night. In the morning that follows this communication, you would then hear the analysts saying that they found this or that particular intriguing report while surfing the Internet during their nocturnal visit to the bathroom.

The importance of being up to date increases as the analysts move through the ranks. Junior analysts are not as involved in the process of identifying new information, and so they are not under so much pressure to always be informed about current developments. For senior analysts, however, being up to date is crucial. In the financial analysis department, I could observe this by the speed of the analysts' movements inside the office. Senior analysts sometimes jog through the office, reflecting the importance of not wasting any time while switching from their own screen to another information source. The faster you move, the more important you are. Lower-ranking analysts are expected to step aside when senior analysts approach in a hurry.

Jonas, the head of the stock market analysis team, was known for his fast and assertive walk. If other analysts wanted to ask him something, they usually had to follow him on his way, talking to his back. Jonas's legendary fast walk was a peril to beginners. It was a critical error not to get out of the way when Jonas ran through the office to get a new piece of information about a particular market trend from another source or a subordinate financial analyst. Blocking Jonas's path once would get the beginner a very angry look, blocking it twice would probably cost the beginner his or her job.

In an article on Japanese stock traders, Miyazaki (2003) elaborates on the need of financial market participants to be up to date. In his ethnographic account, Miyazaki argues that the temporal difference between receiving new market information and executing trades in accordance with this new market information creates a sense of being behind among the traders he studied. Their quest to close the gap between the receipt of information and the execution of trades becomes a critical part of how they perceive time and creates a huge amount of pressure for the traders. As Sudo, a former trader who chose to leave the firm that Miyazaki studied, confessed in an interview: "Sometimes I would go to the toilet and come back to my desk to find that my gains had tripled or quadrupled or that I had made huge losses. When I thought that I had devoted myself to this kind of profession, I felt empty" (quoted in Miyazaki 2003, 260).

Among financial analysts, the engagement with time is slightly different. The primary reason is that, unlike the traders Miyazaki studied, analysts do not directly see the material effect of their use of information. The traders take direct action on timely information, but the analysts create investment advice for other investors to act on. Still, the perception of timeliness as a critical factor in whether information is useful for investment purposes helps to shape what Bear (2014a, 2014b) calls the social rhythms of capital. Among the financial analysts at Swiss Bank, these rhythms in time are formed by the hope of identifying information before it enters the price, by the fear of missing out on relevant information, and by the physical performance of being up to date, such as permanently observing market movements or adopting a fast and assertive walk when moving through the office.

APPLICABILITY

In addition to timeliness, the applicability of information plays an important role in how analysts prioritize information. The easier it is for a source of information to be used to create market forecasts, the higher it is ranked. Market devices such as the Bloomberg and Reuters computer programs deliver information in a highly applicable form. This means that the information they depict often already contain an interpretation of how it could influence financial markets (the information is thus already framed). Moreover, the information coming from these devices often indicates a link to specific companies, economic sectors, or market regions. This is advantageous because, in addition to receiving a piece of information, analysts also get an indication of how the information could affect financial markets.

Identifying the link between new information and its possible effect on financial markets is one of the most challenging tasks for financial analysts. Often, there is a consensus about the importance of a particular news item, but not about the way it will affect financial markets. In spring 2012, for example, when François Hollande was elected president of France, no analyst doubted that the election would affect the stock market in some way. Analysts could not agree, however, on whether Hollande's election would be positive or negative for French companies. Some of the analysts argued that the expected rise in taxes would harm the entire French economy, including domestic companies traded on the stock market. Other analysts disagreed, saying that the protectionist measures that Hollande might introduce could harm the broader economic environment but boost the domestic market. The issue is thus not really to find out whether a new piece of information has an effect on the market, but rather to identify how this effect will play out. Sources that link information to potential market implications are extremely important.

Because of their applicability, reports from sell-side analysts are highly ranked by buy-side analysts. Sell-side analysts write specialized reports that, in addition to data, usually contain a list of possible market implications. At Swiss Bank, the buy-side analysts had access to the reports and services of about ten sell-side analyst teams (including Swiss Bank's own sell-side team). Sell-side analysts usually do not produce analyses for the whole market but concentrate on single sectors and topics, in which they try to build up expertise and a good reputation. To attract attention, their reporting style can be very creative. In one case, a sell-side analyst's investment reports were even inspired by anthropology. A prominent broker used to send around e-mails with ethnographic-style observations from Arabic and African countries with high economic growth, calling them notes from the field.

For their regular reports (which constitute their work, aside from e-mail communication and short-term investment ideas), sell-side analysts sometimes spend months on the research and writing process. It is not unusual for the outcome of a study to be more than one hundred pages. Buy-side analysts rarely read more than ten pages of these reports. They highly appreciate them, however, because the reports can easily be used to produce buy-side analyses that aim to reduce the sell-side studies to a few bullet points that they can then present to clients. Often, the sell-side analysts' reports contain charts and tables, which are then reproduced by the buy-side analysts and

used in their own reports and presentations. Also, they contain a specific view on how to interpret a particular market trend, which can be
adopted by the buy-side analysts.

Marcel, a senior analyst and strong believer in fundamental analysis, however, disliked the way most analysts used these sell-side reports. He was convinced that analysts should base their opinions on
their own estimations, rather than being influenced by the opinion of
other analysts. To look at other reports, Marcel claimed, contradicted
the core principles of fundamental analysis and led to herding behavior. Marcel therefore banned the members of his team, which con-
sisted of four junior analysts, from communicating with the sell-side
analysts and reading their reports. At Swiss Bank, everyone laughed
about Marcel's approach, because it often resulted in highly inaccu-
rate forecasts. One reason was that the reports of sell-side analysts are
distributed across the whole financial industry. If they appear credible and if buy-side analysts choose to reproduce the sell-side analysts' visions, markets are likely to evolve in the direction indicated by
the sell-side analysts.

If most of the analysts agree on a similar investment outlook, they
talk about a consensus call. On Bloomberg, all analysts can check
what other analysts think about the future development of a particular stock. If there is a consensus among the sell-side analysts, buy-side
analysts are likely to take this consensus into consideration, because
it can become a self-fulfilling prophecy. In ignoring such consensus,
the analysts of Marcel's team often deviated from the dominant perception in the market. When I talked about this issue with the analysts from other teams, they stressed the importance of knowing how
other analysts are predicting the future (which again illustrates how
analysts act as second-order observers). Patrick, a senior analyst responsible for automobile stocks, once made the importance very clear
when he told me that developing forecasts without considering other
opinions is pointless: "Other people need to eventually see that your
forecast is correct," he explained. "Here, fundamental analysis has
its limits. Your analysis needs to be in line with others to become reflected in the market."[4]

The extensive use of sell-side reports in Swiss Bank's financial
analysis department shows that analysts prefer to use information
sources that not only give them pieces of information but also indi-

cate how the information can be interpreted in terms of future market movements. There are, however, situations in which no such applicable information sources exist. The Arab Spring, for instance, created one such situation in which analysts had to produce an interpretation without being able to refer to easily applicable reports or sources (see Leins 2011). In response to the Egyptian revolution in January and February 2011, financial analysts had to construct a way of interpreting the political turmoil in terms of economic implications without being able to refer to the information sources they normally use for their work.

Egypt is part of the region that financial market participants refer to as MENA (Middle East and North Africa). Among the Middle Eastern countries, Egypt is the largest economy, a fact that is mainly due to its large population of more than 90 million people. When the financial crisis began in 2007, many investors started to shift their attention and parts of their wealth toward so-called emerging markets to compensate for the poor performance that resulted from the economic downturn in Europe and the United States. In response to this shift, Swiss Bank created a group of emerging markets experts within the financial analysis department. During the Arab Spring, these analysts then had to come up with interpretative frames for how the Egyptian revolution could eventually affect markets. Because none of these analysts had expertise in the political landscape of Egypt, they established contact with external experts. These experts were politicians or political commentators with an expertise in financial markets who were able to translate political events into a market-friendly language that analysts could work with.

On January 26, the day after the Egyptian uprising, two sell-side analysis teams announced a conference call with political experts. The first involved a briefing by a former US ambassador who had been based in Egypt for a while. The other team announced a Q&A session with a former British prime minister. Their analysis did not reveal more than what was already publicly available. Listening to these conference calls, it soon became obvious that these two people were not primarily important because of their political insights, but rather because of their status as experts who could translate political events into market interpretations. Also, they were of value because the Swiss Bank analysts knew that these experts would talk not only with them but also with many other market participants. This, again, made their interpretation more applicable, because the analysts knew that the experts' interpretation was likely to become dominant in financial market discourse.

Generally speaking, to interpret political events such as the Arab Spring and the French presidential election, or ecological events such as Fukushima, analysts have to gather information outside their usual hunting ground. In so doing, they cannot rely on highly ranked information sources and thus have to create calculative frames of their own, as noted by Beunza and Garud (2007). Events of these kinds, however, do not characterize the majority of the financial analysts' working environments. Most of the time, analysts work with pre-framed information items that they develop further but do not create ex nihilo. Analysts are thus often part of a larger frame-making process that involves sell-side analysts, external experts, financial journalists, market devices, and companies under valuation that frame information by communicating it in a particular way. This situation arises from the fact that these sources provide information in a format that is easier to apply to market forecasts. They therefore create some degree of predictability, in that many other market participants also use them to derive their forecasts.

CREDIBILITY

A third factor analysts use when ranking information sources is the credibility of the sources. Credible sources help to create innovative narratives and at the same time underline the role of the financial analysts as experts. Academic research often is treated as a particularly credible source. At Swiss Bank, a library is located next to the financial analysis department. Swiss Bank's internal library exceeds in size many of the academic libraries I know. About five full-time employees work in the library, making sure that all the significant academic books on finance and the economy are available to Swiss Bank's employees.

In the beginning of my fieldwork, I often spent time in this library, reading some of the classics in economic theory, such as Friedman and Keynes. Beyond these classics, the library holds a considerable number of academic journals, as well as many Swiss and foreign newspapers. It also contains a large number of statistical yearbooks that analysts can use to illustrate economic trends. Analysts who use these sources, especially the academic literature, can make a name for themselves among investors and their colleagues. Because the road from academic data to an investment forecast is long, however, analysts rarely get involved in data mining these sources (see Mars 1998) unless a new and promising trend emerges that needs to be underlined in a credible way to verify its legitimacy.

ESG was one such trend that emerged during my time with Swiss Bank. ESG stands for the integration of environmental (E), social (S), and governance-related (G) data into the selection process of investors' portfolios. Broadly speaking, it can be understood as an outcome of the increasingly moralizing discourse on economic processes that has, to some degree, become dominant in recent years (see, for example, Carrier 2012; Garsten 2012; Maurer 2005; Rajak 2011; Rudnyckyj 2010; Stehr 2008). In financial markets, the trend toward ESG-based investing is driven by the perceived need to reflect this public discourse, as well as by the need to generate new investment styles after the old ones (most important among them speculation on structural and cyclical growth) lost their legitimacy when the financial crisis hit.

ESG-based investing can be understood as a successor to socially responsible investing (SRI). Like ESG, SRI was a considerable trend that focused on social and ecological responsibility. Although the approaches used in SRI rarely differed substantially from ESG-based investing, the term "socially responsible investing" disappeared from the agenda of many large banks after a while. Andy and Marco, who were responsible for publishing reports for investors interested in SRI at Swiss Bank, told me that the big banks stopped using the term SRI because the concept proved to be "too normative." As Patrick, an analyst not directly involved in SRI explained, many banks eventually realized that they are supposed to be "a bank, not a church."

SRI was criticized as being too moralistic, but ESG-based investing seemed to represent a more market-friendly model that focuses on raw data rather than on a holistic vision on how the market ought to be. I first heard about ESG in a meeting with sell-side analysts from a famous Wall Street bank in September 2010. Two sell-side analysts, both of them under thirty years old and very nervous, presented their sustainability framework to about four buy-side analysts in one of the client meeting rooms at Swiss Bank. With their framework, the sell-side analysts aimed to combine two levels of analysis in order to come up with what they called a sustainable market view. On the one hand, they stressed the role of conventional fundamental analysis. On the other, they analyzed ESG data by defining a number of environmental, social, and governance-related issues attached to the businesses of publicly listed corporations. In so doing, they stressed that using ESG is not about trying to become "do-gooders" (they said this in a very dismissive tone), but about being able to anticipate what non-economic information could eventually materialize in the markets or hurt a company's reputation. Because they considered only companies that also performed very well in terms of fundamental analysis, they came up with some rather surprising recommendations. According to their framework, companies such as BHP Billiton, HSBC, Roche, and ABB were said to be the "sustainable winners" and thus to be recommended to all investors focused on ESG factors.

During the meeting, it became clear to me that sustainability here meant something radically different from what investors probably meant when asking for sustainable investment recommendations. Sustainability was not being used to describe environmental or social sustainability, but rather the ability to economically survive critical voices coming from the public. Andy, however, was deeply impressed by the sell-side analysts' framework. After the meeting, he enthusiastically told me that someone had finally managed to harmonize the investors' aim of maximizing financial benefit with the aim of being kind to the environment and society. This, Andy stressed, would help him to sell the idea of ESG-based investing to investors who were concerned about society and the environment, as well as to the ones who were interested only in financial gains. As Richard, the head of the financial analysis department and similarly enthusiastic about ESG, later stressed, ESG indicated that "doing good" would no longer necessarily exclude "doing well."

In summer 2010, only a few people inside the financial analysis department had heard of ESG as a market trend. Soon afterward, however, the topic became increasingly popular and was continuously mentioned in the *Financial Times* and on Bloomberg. ESG promised a new style of analysis and investing by integrating environmental, social, and governance-related considerations into stock selection.

At Swiss Bank, ESG was soon recognized as a promising marketing tool for attracting new clients interested in sustainable forms of investment. To produce background research that justified ESG-based investing, a group of about five analysts, including myself, was tasked with developing a framework for how to use ESG data in the everyday working processes of financial analysis. This exercise differed a great deal from what the analysts do when they valuate companies or interpret political and social trends, as the aim was not to produce an investment report, but rather a justification of a new investment style.

To tackle this exercise of producing a publication that justified ESG, many analysts switched to a much more academic style of doing research. Andy started to go through all the new academic books and studies on integrating ESG data into financial analysis. He summarized the books and studies and presented their results to the group. In so doing, he paid particular attention to the findings that supported the hypothesis that taking ESG data into account tends to help investors financially outperform the market. He stressed that these studies could be mentioned in the publication to "make a positive case."

Tobias, an analyst trained in political science and macroeconomics, brought in his personal laptop with the statistics programs he used as a student and started to engage in statistical computation. This project had a different time frame and rhythm of doing analysis than research on immediate stock market developments. Timeliness and applicability became less important, but the approach had to be credible. The team thus used academic literature, studies, and their own statistical findings to underline the credibility of their publication.

New trends such as ESG-based investing make the ranking of credible information sources visible. Credible information is, however, generally of importance to analysts. Every now and then, analysts like to refer to an article in *Harvard Business Review* or to a current academic study to underline their investment forecasts. In so doing, they reinforce their status as experts and stress the empirical foundation of their investment narrative.

ORIGINALITY

At times, originality becomes a fourth requirement when selecting information for use in constructing forecasts. If analysts use information that has not already been used by other analysts, they can promote their forecasts as unique and innovative. The interplay between the use of information that is considered applicable and the use of information that is considered original is particularly interesting. On the one hand, financial analysts know that by using information sources that many other analysts also use, they reduce their chances of coming up with a forecast that is completely against the actual market trend (see Marcel's story in the preceding section on applicability). On the other hand, analysts are aware that their investment reports also are a way of entertaining clients and of stressing their *individual* ability to understand market movements.

When he was introducing me to financial analysis, Marco therefore continually stressed the importance of integrating surprising elements into financial analysis. As he told me, clients have many ways of accessing financial market data. Television shows, newspapers, and specialized magazines offer investors scope for informing themselves about current developments and possible future developments in the market. In this economy of attention—that is, an economy in which actors compete for attention, rather than monetary profit—financial analysts have to come up with original statements and data to catch an investor's attention. In so doing, they will make names for themselves among investors and within the financial analyst community.

Many of the analysts at Swiss Bank had their own strategies for integrating original and surprising data into their reports. William, for example, often referred to studies from political science and sociology as a way of integrating unconventional data into his reports. As a graduate of Oxford's politics, philosophy, and economics master's program, William had a remarkable knowledge in these fields, which he sporadically used for his forecasts. Often, he started his reports by referring to studies done outside economics. Later, however, he usually moved on to information sources whose legitimacy was based on timeliness, applicability, and credibility.

Unusual and surprising sources of information are thus often used to gain the attention of the readers. As Marco used to tell all the analysts when reviewing their reports, the first paragraph of a written report should surprise and intrigue readers and make them want to continue reading. Coming up with original data also helps analysts gain a reputation among other analysts. As Beunza and Garud (2007) state, financial analysis is about fame as much as it is about accuracy. By introducing unconventional data and narratives, financial analysts can become star analysts (Beunza and Garud 2007, 30). Always keeping in line with other analysts' views will reduce the risk of deviating too far from the actual market development. In so doing, however, analysts will not be able to achieve the fame that will increase their popularity and recognition among investors and other analysts.

During my time in the field, the importance of using information that is considered original became evident in the case of Greg, a very popular sell-side analyst from a British investment bank. Greg called himself a senior political analyst and specialized in geopolitical conflicts. When tensions between Israel and Iran arose in 2011, he became famous for estimating and then communicating that there was a 70 percent chance of Israel executing a military strike against Iran by June. Greg did not reveal how he arrived at this figure. Talking to the analysts of Swiss Bank, however, he referred to his connections to the secret services as an original source to which other analysts had no access. Greg knew very well how to communicate forecasts in a way that would gain attention. By linking a future scenario to an original source and an exact time frame, his forecast seemed more original and applicable than others.

Like Greg, many buy-side analysts try to come up with surprising statements about the future in order to raise their profile. To do so, they have to search for and work with information sources that offer originality rather than applicability. Academic publications are among the written sources of information that can offer surprising data. Much of the data that is considered original, however, is collected during personal meetings and talks with experts outside Swiss Bank. Analysts who represent a big brand like Swiss Bank have an advantage because the experts are likely to talk with them. During my time at Swiss Bank, I took part in numerous meetings with experts such as government ministers, renowned academics, and CEOs of large companies.

During these meetings, analysts hoped to gather original information that could not be accessed by simply looking at conventional market data. The problem, however, is that analysts can use only information that is, at least in theory, also available to other market participants, because otherwise it could be considered insider information. Chris, the analyst responsible for pharmaceutical research at Swiss Bank, made great use of his personal network to search for original information that he could use to surprise the recipients of his investment reports. As the holder of a PhD and a former university researcher in pharmaceutics, Chris had a large network of people who were either involved in academic studies or working for pharmaceutical companies in the private sector. By meeting these people regularly, he knew about the latest research and the results of studies that might affect the performance of certain pharmaceutical companies.

For Chris to use this information for his forecasts, however, it at least had to have been published in a scientific journal or discussed at a public event. As soon as the availability of the latest news on the testing of a particular drug (such as possible side effects or promising outcomes) happened, Chris would provide investors with new and often surprising information on the pharmaceutical sector. In so doing, his value as an analyst increased dramatically. Chris's ability to present timely and original information made him one of the most popular and respected analysts at Swiss Bank.

Using original data is important because it allows analysts and investors to develop a specific and apparently unique perspective on financial market movements. As I mentioned, originality is crucial to the work of financial analysts, because providing an apparently unique perspective makes investors feel as if they have been given tools that will help them navigate the highly uncertain and unstable field of financial markets. By listening to Chris, investors received an original interpretation of market movements that they could either accept or decline. His forecasts thus represented a reference point[5] in an uncertain environment and created a sense of agency for other market participants.

The Construction of an
Investment Narrative

In the first weeks of my fieldwork, Marco told me how I could create a market forecast. First, he advised me to take some time getting a "feeling" for how markets work. "This takes a lot of time," Marco explained, "but basically, you just have to observe the market and read financial newspapers and the reports of other analysts." Marco then stared off into space, groping for words. After a while, he said, "You know, it's not just about observing and reading, it's about . . ." He did not finish his sentence. Obviously, he could not put into words how one should develop that feeling for the market he was talking about. "You know, it's about . . . ," Marco made a gesture as if he were touching a very smooth fabric to check whether it was made of silk. "That feeling," he continued, "is what differentiates a good analyst from a bad one." He paused, then continued with a smile: "However, you are a social anthropologist, so I don't expect you to have a problem engaging with feelings."[1]

When I later asked Michael, an analyst working in Marco's team, whether he could walk me through the process of creating a forecast, he was at first reluctant to do so. He pointed to the fact that the creation of predictions cannot be learned as a step-by-step approach but has to result from individual market observation. When I told him that it was important for me to understand how more experienced analysts cope with calculative approaches, he agreed. One morning, Michael came over to my workstation, asking me whether I wanted to watch him create a forecast. One company that Michael covered as an analyst had just reported its latest financial results and Michael was supposed to come up with an adjusted target price based on the company's current financial standing.

I went over to Michael's work station and we looked at the recently reported numbers of the company that were displayed on one of the two computer screens at Michael's workstation. On the other screen, Michael had already prepared a spreadsheet with a handful of calculation formulas. First, Michael looked at the financial results presented in the company's quarterly financial statement. After having studied them, Michael entered them into the spreadsheet, which then calculated a number of coefficients and possible target prices. While entering the numbers, Michael looked at the various formulas' results. Michael seemed to be generally satisfied with the outcome and mentioned from time to time that the resulting numbers displayed on one of his computer screens "generally supported his feeling."

After Michael filled in all the numbers, he took a short rest to look at them and think about how to interpret the results of the various calculative approaches. After staring at them for about five seconds, Michael sighed. Then, he turned to me and started a conversation about the lack of accuracy of many of the estimations that were part of these calculative formulas. After a while, Michael then said in a decisive tone: "You know what, I'll take the most bullish target price and adjust the projections on the overall market development a little. After that, I'll have a target price that truly reflects my feeling about the future development of this particularly promising stock."

As Michael's approach shows, affect plays a critical role in the construction of market forecasts. As Lépinay and Hertz (2005) and Zaloom (2006, 2009) have shown, the same is true for trading. Referring to the work of Keynes (1936), Zaloom (2009, 245) states that, in financial markets, "affect arises when knowledge has no solid ground" (see also Holmes and Marcus 2005; Richard and Rudnyckyj 2009). As Michael's example indicates, affect and calculation become closely intertwined when analysts aim to predict the future. Many times, analysts even choose a calculative strategy *only after* they already have an affect-based strategy in mind.

As Michael's process for estimating the target price confirms, calculative approaches are used in combination with affective elements, which analysts refer to as market feeling. The interaction between numbers and overall strategic perspective is complex and closely intertwined. The role of numbers in financial analysis can take three forms. First, they can be understood as pure signals that tell the analysts something about the present and future state of a company. This corresponds to an economic perspective, in which information is seen as the basis for the imagining of economic futures. Second, numbers can be used to reaffirm affective assumptions. This is what financial analysts refer to as data mining, in which the analyst has a particular view of how a company, sector, or geographic region might develop and thus starts to search for numerical data to support that initial feeling. Third, numbers can be used to signal expertise. In this case, the numbers do not contribute to the construction of a narrative at all. Instead, the numbers are used for the sole purpose of highlighting the analyst's role as an expert.

The different uses of numbers can be exemplified by the analysts' application of the P/E ratio. The P/E ratio is a ratio that compares the stock price (P) of a company to its earnings (E). Put simply, it is used to calculate how much an investor needs to pay per stock in relation to the company's earnings per share of stock. The attraction of calculating the P/E ratio is that it gives investors a very simple scale. One company might have a P/E ratio of 23.5, which means that an investor pays US$23.50 per dollar of earnings per share of stock in the company. Another company might have a P/E ratio of 11.2. This means that an investor has to pay US$11.20 for each dollar earned per share of stock in the company. Analysts who use the P/E ratio for valuation would now claim that company 2 is cheaper than company 1, because investors have to pay less for its stock in order to participate in each dollar earned.

For some analysts, the P/E ratio is a starting point in every analysis, and others fully reject it. At Swiss Bank, Patrick and Tobias once engaged in a loud dispute over the use of the P/E ratio in fundamental analysis. Patrick, a very clever and ambitious analyst responsible for the valuation of companies from various business sectors, usually used the P/E ratio as a starting point for his analyses. If a company is traded at a P/E ratio of lower than 10, he argued, this is an invitation for investors to buy, because they will get more for their money than going for an expensive company, that is, a company with a high P/E ratio. Tobias did not agree. He argued that the P/E ratio did not say much about a company's value. He referred to the companies that did not have earnings yet, but whose capital is a convincing idea or a promising outcome from its activity in research and development.

Tobias pointed out that these companies sometimes have a P/E ratio of 100 or more, but might make a lot of money in the future. Patrick mocked him by saying, "Do you mean like in the early 2000s?" He was referring to the dotcom bubble, when companies with no earnings were traded at very high market prices and then eventually collapsed. Both analysts laughed. Their discussion was so loud it attracted other analysts, who started to express their views. Chris said the P/E ratio was probably not helpful in comparing companies from different sectors, but useful for finding out which companies in a single sector are traded at a cheap price. After discussing the pros and cons of the P/E ratio for a while, they agreed that analysts should decide for themselves whether and how to use the P/E ratio in their work.

The dispute between Patrick and Tobias reveals a difference in the use of numbers for the interpretation of market movements. For Tobias, the P/E ratio was no way to derive an interpretation from numbers, but Patrick used the P/E ratio to produce his forecasts. For him and analysts like him, the P/E ratio not only is a calculative approach but also contains a specific signal about how to read markets. By stressing the importance of the P/E ratio, Patrick stressed his view that present earnings are more reliable than estimations of possible future returns. To Patrick, the P/E ratio thus served as a starting point that contributes to the narrative he constructs to make sense of market movements.

A second way of using numbers is to support a narrative that is not necessarily based on a calculative approach but on affect. Financial analysts refer to this process of searching for numbers that support their initial feeling as data mining. For data mining, analysts make use of publicly available data sets, for example, from the United Nations and its specialized agencies, or of data that are provided by financial services such as Bloomberg and Reuters. These financial services supply data that go far beyond the numbers normally used for the calculation of intrinsic value. Using Bloomberg, for example, analysts can look at a company's financial data (such as earnings, growth, and dividend payments), a company's structure (such as the number of employees and shareholders), or a company's news flow. Also, they can assess data about the regional and industrial environment in which a company operates, or data about past scandals, lawsuits, or the company's commitment to environmental and social responsibility. Overall, analysts have almost unlimited amounts of data to mine (see Mars 1998).

Using existing data to support a constructed future scenario, financial analysts often work with time series. Time series visualize past developments and can therefore be used to illustrate possible future scenarios. The problem with this approach is that there are so many data available that analysts will almost always find data that support their constructed forecast. Analysts deliberately avoid limiting themselves to what data they should use for which type of projection. Also, analysts rarely criticize or discuss the way in which data are used when visualizing a narrative. Data mining is way of enriching the analyst's narrative with numbers that are interpreted in a very specific way. In data mining, creativity is usually more important than critical assessment. Once analysts have established an investment narrative, they tend to ignore any data that contradict their view and highlight the data that support it (behavioral economists call this a confirmation bias).

Normative Foundations to the Construction of Narratives

In addition to calculation and affect, gambling strategies help analysts create an expectation of how stock prices might develop. Gambling strategies are based on the assumption that similarities exist between forecasting activities and gambling. The similarities become apparent when financial analysts talk about forecasting market movements. Often analysts use expressions such as playing the market and betting on a stock. Such analogies are omnipresent in the language analysts use to talk to each other. They also feature in many sell-side analysts' reports written by sell-side analysts. Gambling language is rarely ever used, however, when analysts talk to private investors, because it would undermine their expertise and the assumption that they promote sophisticated investing rather than speculative action. As a result, there is a large gap between the language used among analysts and the language used to communicate analyses to investors.

One reason analysts avoid referring to gambling strategies when writing reports is that, after publication, many reports are circulated not only among wealth managers and clients, but often also among journalists. Once a forecast has been published, it is hard for Swiss

Bank to control who has access to it. Therefore, analysts are advised to always avoid using gambling language and referring to anything as being based on feeling rather than fact in written communication with investors. In oral contact with wealth managers and clients, financial analysts do not have to be that strict. In fact, among some of the investors, the use of affect or gambling strategies in the construction of market predictions are an open secret. Some investors may even want to deal with specific analysts precisely because they trust their feeling or because they assume that the analyst will beat the market by sticking to a gambling strategy.

When I talked with analysts about the success and failure of market forecasts, they often used the phrase "sometimes you win, sometimes you lose" to explain the difficulty of predicting the future. As this statement shows, they clearly do not strictly see their market practices as similar to a scientific process, even though a scientific methodology is suggested to the recipients of their investment reports. When Michael first showed me how he comes up with a forecast, he jokingly opened his drawer and showed me a die he had received as a gift from another analyst at Swiss Bank. Instead of pips, the die was marked with a word on each side: buy, hold, sell. Michael took the die, threw it, and jokingly said: "This is how I come up with a forecast."

The establishment of an analyst's forecast also happens via mnemonics that can be used to articulate investment strategies. The analysts often told me that the golden rule for becoming a good analyst is to stick to a single strategy (as I described it in chapter 5, textbooks contain the same golden rule). The strategy chosen usually is supported by mnemonics such as "the trend is your friend" or "buy low, sell high."[2] When analysts refer to the mnemonic "the trend is your friend," they are describing the strategy that says you should always try to benefit from current market trends, regardless of long-term trends. If analysts follow a "buy low, sell high" strategy, they are stressing the importance of not getting vexed by short-term market trends that do not reflect the analyst's original expectations.

The analysts at Swiss Bank often mentioned that these mnemonics help them to avoid being tricked by the market. Therefore, some of them stick to their strategies, even if they are not supported by the actual market development. One rather tragic example of this strong preference for sticking to a strategy was Sébastien's valuation of Solaris. Solaris is a solar energy stock that Sébastien particularly liked. In almost every report and every meeting, Sébastien, who was responsible for the analysis of companies in the alternative energy sector, talked about Solaris as a highly promising stock that he believed would gain in value in the coming years. In 2011, however, the stock price of Solaris started to plummet. Although some of the senior analysts who were in contact with the wealth managers of the bank started to put pressure on Sébastien to downgrade Solaris from a buy recommendation to a hold or even a sell recommendation, Sébastien made it very clear that he did not want to adjust his positive outlook for the stock.

When I talked to Sébastien about that episode, he told me that when the market seems to go against the analyst's feeling, it is particularly important to stay strong. Hence, Sébastien clearly applied a buy low, sell high strategy that he was not willing to adapt for what he considered to be short-term market turbulence. In 2011 Solaris's share price was US$125. In 2012, when the stock price was down to almost US$10, wealth managers and clients holding Solaris in their portfolios started to call Sébastien, asking him for an explanation of the buy rating. As Sébastien told them, he was aware of the current loss. Nevertheless, he explained, he believed Solaris to be a great company with a promising future and so expected the stock to recover at some point. In spring 2012, the pressure from the wealth managers and clients became too much and Sébastien was sanctioned by the department's manager for his false prognosis.

Sébastien's story reveals how far analysts might go in order to stick to their strategy once it is developed. As Sébastien made clear, any deviation from his strategy would have meant being overrun by the market and losing his sense of agency and authority within the market. Again, this importance of sticking to one strategy is reminiscent of casino gamblers who always put their money on red or on odd numbers (Loussouarn 2010; see all contributions in Cassidy, Pisac, and Loussouarn 2013). It expresses the illusion of being able to outsmart the market (or the bank in the casino) by applying a strategy that never changes.

The creation of a sense of agency by understanding market activities as being similar to gambling activities sometimes also materializes in real bets. Every now and then, analysts bet against each other on the future development of financial markets. In so doing, they stress their commitment to their own strategy. All financial analysts agree that there are components in stock market forecasting that cannot be calculated. In order to become good analysts, they thus have to create environments in which they can test expectations and develop strategies. Betting against each other is one way of testing a strategy, and personally engaging in stock market activity is another. An analyst's own investment activity is of course problematic and therefore legally restricted by Swiss Bank. Analysts have a hostile attitude toward this restriction and argue that their own participation in the stock market is an important way of testing their strategies. Marco, for example, was convinced that analysts should invest in the stock market themselves. As he argued, participating in the game is the only surefire way of developing a feeling for the market.

The omnipresence of gambling- and mnemonics-based strategies in Swiss Bank's financial analysis department underlines the degree to which uncertainty features in the financial analysts' profession. To overcome this uncertainty, analysts rely on strategies that help them to make sense of market developments. Gambling strategies and mnemonics are an underlying logic from which investment narratives can be derived and reaffirmed.[3]

In addition to the gambling metaphors and mnemonics, there also is a strong free market narrative[4] that serves as an underlying compass and influences the way financial analysts establish strategies and transform them into investment narratives. The idea of the superiority of the free market serves as an ideological basis that structures analyses and helps analysts interpret current developments. The existence of this ideological framework does not mean that analysts are generally uncritical defenders of capitalism. When discussing current economic issues, I was often surprised at how critical some of them are. When it comes to their analyses of the market, however, they clearly consider any type of regulation to be bad.

In harmony with this attitude, analysts also generally express skepticism about people who operate in the political realm. Many analysts assume that most efforts to regulate markets are based on a lack of understanding of how markets work. Their assumption reveals a culture of smartness, as Ho (2009) calls it. Because smartness is a central concept in the education and recruitment of people who want to work in financial institutions, financial analysts later tend to judge the activities of all other market participants (especially regulators) as originating from a lack of understanding. The antagonistic view that financial analysts take toward any kind of market regulation frequently leads them to ignore political developments in their analyses, despite the fact that gaining an understanding of political developments could help them to decrease the uncertainty they face. This reveals the normative element of neoliberal thought: in this worldview, free markets promote efficiency and growth, and regulation distorts competition.

Reporting Season: From a Strategy to a Stable Narrative

When asked to describe their job, financial analysts usually begin by explaining a number of processes that take place within a very particular time frame: the reporting season. The term "reporting season" designates the four periods within a year during which companies reveal their quarterly financial results. The financial calendar is divided into four quarters, and listed companies publish their financial results at the end of each quarter. The first quarter (referred to as Q1) runs from January to March, the second quarter (Q2) from April to June, the third quarter (Q3) from July to September, and the fourth quarter (Q4) from October to December. The reporting season begins after the end of each quarter in the financial calendar and lasts for about one month. During this time, companies report their quarterly financial results, which financial analysts then integrate into their valuation of the companies. The reporting season often is the time when analysts change their investment advice and adjust their market forecasts. For example, they can upgrade their investment advice on a particular stock from hold to buy or from sell to hold, or they can downgrade them from buy to hold or from hold to sell.

Shortly before the end of each quarter, as well as in the following weeks, activity levels in the financial analysis department increase. During this time, no analyst is allowed to go on vacation and being sick is almost unacceptable. Analysts know in advance what day the companies they cover will report their data. On these days in particular, but essentially throughout the whole reporting season, analysts try to minimize all other activities such as meetings, business lunches, and project-based duties. Although the reporting season is very important for the fundamental stock market analysts, it does not affect some of the other teams in the financial analysis department. Currency and commodity analysts, for example, are not concerned with the reporting season. Their "fundamentals" are created by central bank interventions, political conflicts, and social or environmental events, rather than by the quarterly results of companies. Also, the daily tasks of the IT team, which makes up a considerable part of the financial analysis department at Swiss Bank, are not particularly affected by the reporting season.

Members of the financial analysis department who were not involved in the stock valuation process did not know about the importance of the reporting season for the stock market analysts. This regularly led to conflicts during the time I spent in the department. In summer 2011, for example, I was involved in a large IT project that aimed to update the intranet site of Swiss Bank's financial analysis department. At the time, the depiction of market data on the intranet was incomplete and sometimes even showed outdated stock prices to the clients. In addition, the managers of the financial analysis department decided to provide clients with additional data, primarily about companies' social and environmental performance. During the preparation phase of the project, the IT team was responsible for managing the project agenda. Much to the fundamental analysts' chagrin, the IT team scheduled the testing phase of the new intranet page for the fall reporting season. Analysts protested against the plans, arguing that they did not have time for anything other than following the companies' results during the fall reporting season. They stressed that the reporting season was the most important time for them and that they needed to be fully focused on the numbers and new information being reported by the companies they cover.

As much as fundamental analysts like to be dramatic about their workload, their protestations were in fact no exaggeration, for their long working days become even longer during the reporting season. Laurent, a thirty-three-year-old analyst covering the biotech sector, usually came to work between 7:30 a.m. and 7:45 a.m. During reporting season, however, he never arrived later than 7:00 a.m. He had to be there early, especially on the days when a company he covered reported its numbers. Companies usually report their numbers before the local financial market opens. Thus, in Switzerland they tend to report between 7:00 a.m. and 8:00 a.m. The reason for the practice is to give financial analysts enough time to interpret the numbers before the market opens at 9:00 a.m.[5] The processing of the reported numbers is done collaboratively, but with a strict division of labor. Integrating the numbers into mathematical models is many times delegated to analysts with a lower reputation, such as the KPO analysts in Mumbai or trainees in Zurich. While these less experienced analysts fill in the numbers and do the calculations, the more experienced analysts interpret the figures and construct a persuasive story. They translate strategies that are based on calculation, affect, and normative assumptions into narratives that can be communicated to the investors.

At 9:00 a.m., when the markets open for trading, analysts start to communicate the reported numbers and their interpretation of whether the latest numbers are a good or bad sign for future share prices. Because analysts always try to anticipate future market developments, stock prices do not always simply rise as a result of good numbers or fall as a result of bad numbers. If a company reports high revenues when analysts expected the companies to have high revenues, the revenues appear to be priced in. As a result, the actual reporting of high revenues may have no effect on the stock price at all. What really affects the stock market during the reporting season is a substantial difference between the analysts' expectations and the reported number. Sometimes the difference can lead to a decline in the stock price of a company that just reported high revenues because the analysts expected the revenues to be even higher (and vice versa). In such cases, the journalists use phrases such as "the numbers exceeded analysts' expectations" or "analysts were disappointed by the numbers reported."

The anticipation of quarterly financial results often is fostered by sell-side analysis reports that estimate future reported numbers based on the overall economic development, information on a company's performance that is public before the day of reporting, and projected developments based on results reported in the past. Although sell-side analysts reported such estimations proactively, the analysts at Swiss Bank were much more cautious. During the days before a company reported, they rarely changed the investment recommendation. The reason, as an analyst once told me, is that such prereporting advice could be understood as speculative by individual investors.

Here, the analysts at Swiss Bank normally preferred to wait until the actual reported numbers were out, even if that meant that investors who were acting on their recommendations could not financially exploit estimations and rumors that circulated before the reporting day.

The Company Report

Swiss Bank's financial analysts communicate their market forecasts in various ways, ranging from oral advice or short e-mails to more institutionalized forms. Of the more institutionalized forms, the company report is the most established (see figures 3 and 4 for an exemplary company report).[6] Analysts are expected to write a company report every time a company they cover publishes its numbers or announces a change in strategy. Company reports contain the numbers reported, a variety of other market data, and investment advice that gives investors an idea of how the company's stock price might develop in the future. The content of the company report illustrates how financial analysts interpret and communicate their visions about a company, the overall economy, and the future development of financial markets. Above all, however, it illustrates how financial analysts construct and communicate investment narratives that look coherent and are built to persuade investors. In company reports, analysts use not only text, but also illustrations, charts, and tables. In so doing, they produce reports that look both appealing and sophisticated.

VISUAL APPEARANCE

The design of the company report reveals its primary function. Looking at the report, the reader will most probably first notice the investment recommendation (the large-format "buy" in the example report—figures 3 and 4). Analysts at Swiss Bank have the option of giving one of three recommendations: buy, hold, or sell. A buy recommendation indicates that the analyst thinks that the stock price will rise, and so he or she recommends that investors should buy stocks in that company. A sell recommendation advises investors to sell the stock. A hold recommendation means that the analyst thinks the stock price will remain more or less constant over time. The analyst therefore advises investors who already own the stock to hold it and those who do not, not to buy it.

SWISS BANK

Company Report

Zurich, 25 April 2013
Food Products
Investment Horizon: 6-12+ months
Marcel Meier, Research Analyst
marcel.meier@swiss-bank.ch

Eat-A-Lot Inc.
Strongest growing food products company

Eat-A-Lot is increasingly an emerging market story

Eat-A-Lot is one of the world's largest food products and household & personal care manufacturers with a strong product portfolio and especially the highest emerging market exposure. Over the past few quarters - admittedly some excellent ones - however we have gained confidence that CEO Samuel Burger has started to turn around the company. Our positive view is based on our expectations that Eat-A-Lot will be able to grow sustainably by 3%-5% and further expand its CFROIs to 20%-25% levels.

Expected built-up of a valuation premium vis-à-vis the industry

With another few adjustments to our model, our new target price is EUR 34. It was derived using our DCF model with a 4.5% real cost of capital. Relative to the global food products industry, we now think the valuation gap should further narrow and superior emerging market growth warrants a valuation premium. On the basis of that, we maintain our BUY recommendation.

Eat-A-Lot's organic sales growth pattern seem intact

In its trading statement, Eat-A-Lot reported Q1 2013 organic sales growth of 4.9% which was driven by 2.2% volume growth and price increases of 2.6%. This was slightly weaker than we had anticipated but the strongest in the industry, and therefore does not challenge our investment thesis on Eat-A-Lot, especially as the price/volume mix was fairly pleasing, in our view. Also, though not an excuse, we have to admit that the comparable base of Q1 2012 was fairly high. Regionally, Emerging Markets (+10.4%) grew still outstandingly strong, and the weak spot once again was Western Europe where organic growth was disappointing -3.1% on the back of -2.5% volume growth and price cuts (-1.0%). No formal outlook statement was provided.

Current price: EUR 32.21 / target price: 34.00

BUY Upside potential 5.6%

Highlights

- Eat-A-Lot is increasingly an emerging market story.

- Expected built-up of a valuation premium vis-à-vis the industry.

- Eat-A-Lot's organic sales growth pattern seen intact.

- Eat-A-Lot's food and HPC portfolio is further gaining traction.

- Organic growth to drive operating profit margins.

- Eat-A-Lot faces key challenges to be substantially more successful.

Eat-A-Lot, historical performance

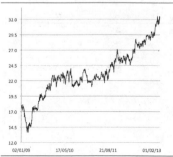

Source: Swiss Bank. Any reference to past performance is not necessarily indicative of future results.

Figure 3. Example of a company report (first page)

Valuation			
Fiscal year-end 12/2013	2012A	2013E	2014E
EPS (EUR)	1.82	1.98	2.12
P/E	n.a.	16.3	15.2
Dividend per share (EUR)	97.00	1.00	1.05
Dividend yield	n.a.	3.1%	3.3%
Book value / share	n.a.	6.4	n.a.
Source: Swiss Bank			

Eat-A-Lot's food and HPC portfolio is further gaining traction

We have been repeatedly positively surprised by the volume trend progression Eat-A-Lot has demonstrated in many of the past quarters, though we think it was also helped by increases in advertising & promotion expenses. Moreover, we believe that CEO Samuel Burger has significantly improved the quality and the growth profile of Eat-A-Lot's product portfolio, also with respect to brand positioning. This should sustain organic growth in Eat-A-Lot's core regions.

Income statement			
EUR m	2012A	2013E	2014E
Net sales	49,383	52,161	54,658
Sales growth	6.3%	5.6%	4.8%
EBITDA	8,620	9,262	9,869
EBITDA-margin	17.5%	17.8%	18.1%
Net income	5,001	5,415	5,802
Source: Swiss Bank			

Organic growth to drive operating profit margins

We now think that Eat-A-Lot's strong organic growth should drive margin progression of at least 20 bp per year, though we continue to believe that Eat-A-Lot's operating profit margins are vulnerable with respect to input costs. Our forecasts for core operating margins are 14.3% for 2013 and 14.5% for 2014. We believe Eat-A-Lot will need to further boost advertising & promotion spending to maintain its market shares and further strengthen its brands to offset cost pressure.

Cash flow statement			
EUR m	2012A	2013E	2014E
Cash flow from operations	6,718	7,200	7,649
Cash flow (before dividends)	5,308	5,715	6,095
Total capex	1,580	1,669	1,749
Capex/sales	3.2%	3.2%	3.2%
Source: Swiss Bank			

Balance sheet			
EUR m	2012A	2013E	2014E
Operating cash	988	1,043	1,093
Net Working Capital (NWC)	-2,515	-2,67	-2,784
Net Property, Plant & Equipment (PP&E)	8,975	9,596	10,252
Total assets	47,438	51,558	54,637
Common equity	18,096	20,706	22,298
Net debt	5,719	2,814	934
Net debt/equity	0.3	0.1	0.0
Source: Swiss Bank			

Eat-A-Lot faces key challenges to be substantially more successful

Eat-A-Lot currently generates about 54.4% of sales (2013E) in emerging markets, particularly with household & personal products, and is extremely successful there, particularly in terms of product positioning. In Western Europe, however, although it has made some progress over the past few quarters with respect to market shares, the situation remains very challenging as consumer sentiment is subdued and is likely to remain so. However, we acknowledge the excellent track record Samuel Burger has and the excellent work he has done at Eat-A-Lot, but we stick to our earlier view that even he will need much more time to completely turn around Eat-A-Lot in Europe and introduce true innovation and blockbusters to boost Eat-A-Lot going forward.

Relative to industry benchmark

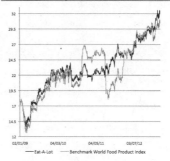

02/01/09　　04/03/10　　04/05/11　　03/07/12

— Eat-A-Lot　　— Benchmark World Food Product Index

Source: Swiss Bank. Any reference to past performance is not necessarily indicative of future results.

Figure 4. Example of a company report (second page)

Institutions vary in the terminology they use to give investment advice. Other analysts prefer the expressions "overweight" (investors should buy) and "underweight" (investors should sell). Some use more detailed categories, including "strong buy" and "strong sell." To make the investment advice look more sophisticated, Swiss Bank's report also prominently displays a so-called upside (or downside) potential. In addition to the ternary recommendation system, the inclusion of the percentage upside potential allows readers to imagine a potential future win or loss.

In addition to the investment recommendation and the target price, six bullet points, presented as highlights, are placed prominently on the first page of the report. The bullet points conveniently list the main characteristics of an analyst's storyline. As figures 3 and 4 show, they do not in fact give specific data or calculative strategies. Rather, they are written in such a way as to make the recipient of the report read the full story.

Before a company report is published, it needs to be reviewed by at least two people. The first reviewer is always a financial analyst, who checks whether the narrative is consistent. The second reviewer is never a financial analyst, but a person with specific training in language editing and communication. During the two years I was with Swiss Bank, these second reviewers and the analysts discussed and amended the title of the reports and the bullet points on numerous occasions. Although the reviewers responsible for language editing and communication usually argued that the title and the bullet points were the most important elements of the report, not all the analysts were necessarily willing to adapt their way of writing and presenting their investment narrative.

Particularly for the analysts who joined Swiss Bank after having earned a PhD, the need to break down their analysis into simple highlights sometimes created a problem. Sébastien once told me how he was uncomfortable with always having to reduce complex information to simple statements. At the university, he argued, people are not trained to simplify complex information, but in the market economy it is all about reducing complex information to simple market signals. Other analysts, such as Patrick, did not have a problem with creating simple statements to express complex issues. Often analysts with the ability to do so used it to discredit the analysts with PhDs. Patrick, for example, once told me that a PhD might be a good way of acquiring expertise, but it is never a guarantee that someone will be a good analyst. Sometimes, he claimed, it even prevents people from being good analysts because they get too involved in complex analyses and do not concentrate on putting their analyses into simple narratives that are easy to understand.

In addition to the buy, hold, or sell recommendation and the target price and the highlights, every company report has one chart on the first page. Usually, the chart depicts a development in the stock price of the company discussed in the report. Although the reviewers responsible for language editing and communication usually give feedback on the title and the bullet points, it is the first reviewers who usually evaluate the chart. The visualization of market developments through charts is considered to be very important because it supports the narrative. The chart is always constructed in a way that ensures that it serves the overall investment narrative.

In the case of a buy recommendation, the analysts specifically engineer the charts to make them look convincing. When constructing the chart, analysts have many options for visualizing the data in a way that supports their narrative. They can freely choose what time frame and what unit of scale they use for the construction of a chart. Analysts can select a very particular time frame or scale in order to make the chart look convincing. The example report in figures 3 and 4 displays this kind of engineered chart. By choosing January 2009 as the starting point for the historical data, a point in time when the global financial market hit a low point, the analyst produced a picture of a very strong increase in the stock price. Choosing a different starting point would have revealed that the post-2009 growth in Eat-A-Lot's stock price was much more the result of a general recovery phase after the global economic downturn than the outcome of a growth pattern, as the analyst claims in the report. Also, cutting the scale of the chart at a price of US$12 makes the increase look much more dramatic. On a scale from US$0 to US$40, the visual trend line would have been much less impressive (see figure 5).

The analysts do not see this creative and experimental way of dealing with and visualizing data as problematic because they know that the investment narrative itself is not strictly based on data, but on an eclectic approach. The ability to work creatively with data and to construct convincing charts is thus a highly respected skill among the analysts. After a report was published, the others analysts often would discuss it. If they felt that an analyst had managed to produce a particularly convincing chart, they usually showed their admiration for the achievement. Instead of questioning the substance and use of the data, they complimented the analyst on managing and visualizing the data in a persuasive way.

NARRATIVE STRUCTURE

In the first paragraph, Marcel, the author of the exemplary report, gives a broader context on the company Eat-A-Lot. He expresses his belief that market exposure to so-called emerging markets is the key to the future growth of the company. Also, Marcel expresses his belief in Samuel Burger, Eat-A-Lot's CEO. His "confidence" is not based on the CEO's specific strategy but on the past results, which were "excellent." Marcel uses a strategy of personalization by stressing the role that the CEO plays in Eat-A-Lot's performance. The CEO certainly plays an important role in defining the strategy of the firm, and it also is a good way of making the story about people, rather than just about numbers.

Paragraph 1: Eat-A-Lot is increasingly an emerging market story

Eat-A-Lot is one of the world's largest food products and household & personal care manufacturers with a strong product portfolio and especially the highest emerging market exposure. Over the past few quarters—admittedly some excellent ones—however we have gained confidence that CEO Samuel Burger has started to turn around the company. Our positive view is based on our expectations that Eat-A-Lot will be able to grow sustainably by 3%–5% and further expand its CFROIs to 20%–25% levels.

After presenting a short outline of the investment narrative, Marcel introduces a second element: the justification of the estimation of the future stock price. Here, he switches from a context-based to a calculation-based line of argumentation, setting out percentages for growth and introducing a calculative approach, the CFROI. By introducing this specific calculative valuation model, Marcel links the per-

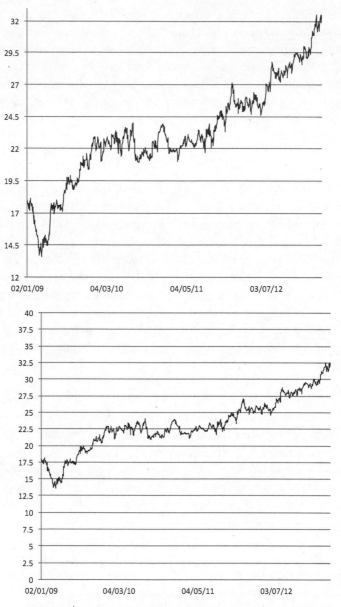

Figure 5. Engineering of the historical performance chart. *Above*: Chart as shown on company report versus chart with larger scale (US$0 to US$40). *Opposite*: Chart as shown on company report versus chart with shorter time frame (January 2011–present).

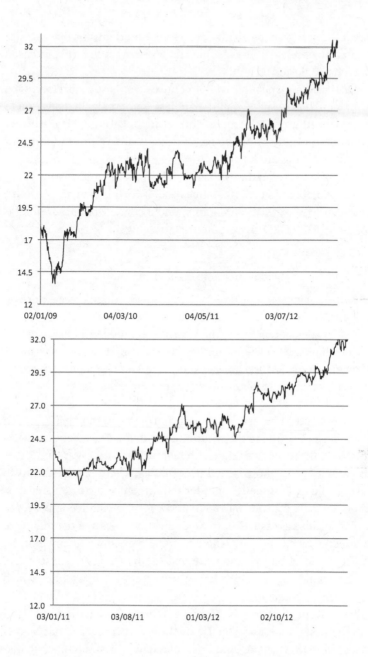

Upper chart:

y-axis: 32, 29.5, 27, 24.5, 22, 19.5, 17, 14.5, 12

x-axis: 02/01/09, 04/03/10, 04/05/11, 03/07/12

Lower chart:

y-axis: 32.0, 29.5, 27.0, 24.5, 22.0, 19.5, 17.0, 14.5, 12.0

x-axis: 03/01/11, 03/08/11, 01/03/12, 02/10/12

sonalized narrative to calculation. This strengthens his line of argumentation because it implies that the investment narrative is based on both people and on numbers.

As in all company reports, Marcel uses words such as *expectation* and *assumption* to signal that the analyst is not really in a position to foresee the future development. This terminology is important, in that it protects the author from being held responsible if the development does not occur as predicted. At the end of the paragraph, Marcel reiterates that the estimation is based not simply on crude assumption, but on a combination of calculative models (in this case, the CFROI), a projection of growth estimations, and a context-based interpretation (role of the CEO, importance of emerging markets).

Paragraph 2: Expected built-up of a valuation premium vis-à-vis the industry

With another few adjustments to our model, our new target price is EUR 34. It was derived using our DCF model with a 4.5% real cost of capital. Relative to the global food products industry, we now think the valuation gap should further narrow and superior emerging market growth warrants a valuation premium. On the basis of that, we maintain our BUY recommendation.

The second paragraph is a description of the methodical approach Marcel used to develop the recommendation to buy stocks in Eat-A-Lot. Here, the reciprocal relationship between numbers and interpretation that I pointed out before becomes apparent. Marcel admits to having adjusted his model in order to harmonize the calculated outcome with the broader narrative and other calculative approaches (which in this case is DCF). In this adjustment we see the influence of affect, which is at work when defining a possible outcome of the forecast calculated by a model. Because Marcel has to substantiate his expectation, however, he links the expectation to a model, which he says he adjusted.

Later in this paragraph, Marcel refers to a "valuation gap" and a "valuation premium." The use of these terms reveals that Marcel bases his analysis on the fundamental analysts' assumption that analysts can detect a difference between a company's intrinsic value and its market value. The valuation gap is the difference between these two values. Marco believes the "valuation gap should further narrow," which means that he expects the market price to slowly adjust to what he considers to be the "intrinsic value" of the company.

After having given a broader context and introduced the calculative approaches used, Marcel focuses on the company's economic performance, rather than on the performance of the company's stock. This is a classic approach used by fundamental analysts, for they believe the basis for the intrinsic value is to be found in a company's business fundamentals, such as volume growth and price increase. Paragraph 3 aims to legitimize the forecast and signal expertise:

Paragraph 3: Eat-A-Lot's organic sales growth pattern seem intact

In its trading statement, Eat-A-Lot reported Q1 2013 organic sales growth of 4.9% which was driven by 2.2% volume growth and price increases of 2.6%. This was slightly weaker than we had anticipated but the strongest in the industry, and therefore does not challenge our investment thesis on Eat-A-Lot, especially as the price/volume mix was fairly pleasing, in our view. Also, though not an excuse, we have to admit that the comparable base of Q1 2012 was fairly high. Regionally, Emerging Markets (+10.4%) grew still outstandingly strong, and the weak spot once again was Western Europe where organic growth was disappointing –3.1% on the back of –2.5% volume growth and price cuts (–1.0%). No formal outlook statement was provided.

Marcel uses many numbers and ratios to support the investment narrative. Also, he points out the problem of calculating the stock's future price by comparing the current price to the past price. He mentions that last year's results (Q1 2012) were comparably high, which could weaken the promising outlook of the stock. In so doing, Marcel takes an active role in interpreting the numbers and reflects on his perception instead of just repeating calculation-based results. This positioning of the analyst as the one who has the epistemological authority to interpret numbers is of crucial importance. In addition to giving an investment recommendation based on numbers, the investment report also aims to affirm the status of the analyst as an expert. By demonstrating his expertise, Marcel can position himself as an individual who understands the movements of the market.

In the fourth paragraph, Marcel returns to the personal dimension of the investment narrative. He again mentions his faith in the company's CEO as a person and strategist, and thus reinforces his enthusiasm about the firm as an opportunity for investors. Building on the earlier paragraphs that focused on Eat-A-Lot as a traded stock (second paragraph) and on the economic parameters of the company (third paragraph), Marcel now elaborates on the company's business model. He talks about how the company has increased its activities in advertising and promoting the brand, and about how this effort has resulted in better brand positioning. Marcel thus shows that, in addition to knowing about the company's financial standing and its market value, he also has a specific insight into the company's strategy. It is interesting that Marcel does not tell the reader where his insights come from. He could have gained them from talking to representatives of the firm, from a newspaper article, or from a sell-side analyst.

Paragraph 4: Eat-A-Lot's food and HPC
portfolio is further gaining traction

We have been repeatedly positively surprised by the volume trend progression Eat-A-Lot has demonstrated in many of the past quarters, though we think it was also helped by increases in advertising & promotion expenses. Moreover, we believe that CEO Samuel Burger has significantly improved the quality and the growth profile of Eat-A-Lot's product portfolio, also with respect to brand positioning. This should sustain organic growth in Eat-A-Lot's core regions.

The last two paragraphs (paragraphs 5 and 6) do not introduce any new perspectives. Instead, they repeat the established narrative and its justification. Unlike the preceding paragraphs, however, they are more critical and even contain suggestions for the company itself. ("We believe Eat-A-Lot will need to further boost advertising & promotion spending to maintain its market share and further strengthen its brand to offset cost pressure.") Readers may wonder why this kind of strategic advice appears in the investment report. The reason is that companies themselves rely heavily on the ratings that the analysts produce. Swiss Bank is a large corporation, and so a positive investment recommendation can have a positive effect on Eat-A-Lot's stock market value. The analysts can thus increase their influence by articulating strategic ideas for the company in their investment reports. In this way analysts clearly become important actors in the governing process of the market, in that they have the opportunity to shape markets as well as describe them.

Paragraph 5: Organic growth to drive operating profit margins

We now think that Eat-A-Lot's strong organic growth should drive margin progression of at least 20 bp per year, though we continue to believe that Eat-A-Lot's operating profit margins are vulnerable with respect to input costs. Our forecasts for core operating margins are 14.3% for 2013 and 14.5% for 2014. We believe Eat-A-Lot will need to further boost advertising & promotion spending to maintain its market shares and further strengthen its brands to offset cost pressure.

Paragraph 6: Eat-A-Lot faces key challenges
to be substantially more successful

Eat-A-Lot currently generates about 54.4% of sales (2013E) in emerging markets, particularly with household & personal products, and is extremely successful there, particularly in terms of product positioning. In Western Europe, however, although it has made some progress over the past few quarters with respect to market shares, the situation remains very challenging as consumer sentiment is subdued and is likely to remain so. However, we acknowledge the excellent track record Samuel Burger has and the excellent work he has done at Eat-A-Lot, but we stick to our earlier view that even he will need much more time to completely turn around Eat-A-Lot in Europe and introduce true innovation and blockbusters to boost Eat-A-Lot going forward.

In sum, three elements are particularly important in the construction of an investment narrative. First, analysts need to deal with calculative approaches and reported numbers in a way that recipients of their forecast will accept them as experts in the market. Second, analysts need to support their storyline with narrative and visualization techniques. Here, translating data into charts, figures, and tables is of importance. Third, in addition to referring to numbers and data, analysts also need to show that their investment narrative is based on more than just calculation. At this point, they often refer to personal elements, unexpected data, and background information. This allows them to reinforce their agency as individual market experts. By stressing that their approach is individual rather than collective, the analysts can present themselves not only as executers of learned processes, but as "charismatic seers" (Bear 2015) who can interpret market movements in a way other market participants cannot.[7]

The Politics of
Circulating Narratives

After being constructed, investment narratives are circulated at Swiss Bank. Circulation aims to achieve two goals. First, the investment narratives are distributed to asset managers and client advisers (both subcategories of wealth managers), as well as to actively investing clients, who use them as tools for navigating through the uncertainties of the market. Within this process, financial analysts have an intermediary role. They are situated between actual market developments and market actors seeking interpretations (see Beunza and Garud 2007). The circulation of narratives at Swiss Bank normally follows two paths. First, they circulate between financial analysts, asset managers, and institutional clients. Second, they circulate between financial analysts, client advisers, and individual clients (see figure 6). There are also close relationships between the financial analysts and the host bank and between the analysts and external media and the public. I elaborate on these latter relationships in chapter 8.

Second, through the circulation of the investment narratives, responsibility for the outcome of investment decisions is disseminated among the various groups of actors involved in making investment decisions. Financial analysts create investment narratives, wealth managers suggest making investments on the basis of these narratives, and clients invest according to the advice given by the wealth managers. All three parties thus become involved in and bear responsibility for the decision on how money is invested. If an investment results in a loss, the *dissemination of responsibility* can become an advantage to the parties involved. They can externalize failure and blame it on the other parties and thereby retain confidence in their own investment narratives.

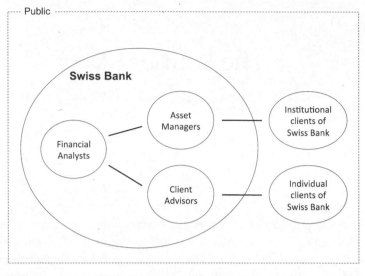

Figure 6. Analysts as intermediaries

The Politics of Narratives in Asset Management

One of the tasks performed by Swiss Bank's financial analysts is to produce market visions and price forecasts for use by Swiss Bank's asset managers. Asset managers are responsible for managing Swiss Bank's own funds and the large portfolios of institutional clients. Institutional clients are nonindividual clients, such as pension funds, smaller companies, and family businesses. Asset managers are thus in charge of large amounts of money, especially in Switzerland, where much of the mandatory pension payments are invested in such funds. When investing this money in the market, asset managers select stocks, bonds, and other financial products on behalf of institutional clients. In so doing, they use the market expertise and the predictions made by the in-house financial analysts to decide which investment vehicles to choose in order to maximize the performance of a fund or portfolio.

Asset managers communicate with the analysts in various ways. They receive the analysts' written company reports and are informed by e-mail whenever financial analysts think that a particular market development could affect an asset manager's investment strategy.

Also, asset managers meet financial analysts regularly. Normally, the financial analysts go to the offices of the asset managers, which are a fifteen-minute walk from the financial analysts' department. The fact that the analysts visit the asset managers, and not the other way around, tells us something about the relationship between these two groups. Financial analysts see themselves as providers of a service to the asset managers. Each meeting or discussion with asset managers is reported to Swiss Bank's management to show that the services they provide are utilized and appreciated by the asset managers. This is because, although many individual clients rely on the financial analysts' expertise as a unique source of market interpretations, asset managers are professionals with plenty of access to alternative analyses.

One important difference between the work of financial analysts and the work of asset managers is that, unlike the analysts' task, which primarily consists of constructing and promoting their narratives, the asset managers' task is to increase financial returns for their clients. This difference has a huge impact on the relationship between analysts and asset managers and influences the way in which they interact. From their experience, asset managers know that adopting and acting according to the narratives of financial analysts is just one way of trying to generate financial return. Therefore, they normally consider other sources of information and other investment strategies to try to maximize financial gains. For example, they also get investment reports of analysts from other banks (sell-side financial analysis reports) and work with valuation models themselves. They have their own Bloomberg stations and often combine the analysts' views with their own perspective on the market. This is something that financial analysts do not like to see, in that it undermines their influence.

During the time I was with Swiss Bank, there were numerous discussions about the purpose of giving asset managers their own valuative freedom. Richard, the head of the financial analysis department repeatedly stated that the advice from financial analysis should *automatically* flow into the portfolio selection of Swiss Bank's asset management, without giving asset managers the freedom to apply other valuation strategies. Recognizing the opportunity to increase their influence, all the analysts supported Richard's claim. The introduction of an automatic selection process based on the analysts' recommendation to buy, hold, or sell a stock would have represented a massive expansion of the power that Swiss Bank's analysts have inside the company.

Although financial analysts strived to increase their influence over asset managers' selection processes, asset managers wanted to continue to be able to choose their sources of information themselves. Internally, they often complained about the lack of quality of in-house analyses and called for additional personnel in asset management so that they could do valuations themselves. Although I did experience examples of productive cooperation between financial analysts and asset managers, the relationship between them was rather competitive overall. Often, asset managers criticized the financial analysts for not really understanding the client.

The tension between the roles became very clear during a meeting I attended with a number of asset managers and financial analysts who were interested in environmentally and socially responsible investment strategies. Everyone at the meeting agreed that Swiss Bank should offer clients a selection of what they called responsible investment opportunities. Discussions then turned to a concept for selecting these firms. Immediately, the financial analysts offered to develop a concept that could later be used by the asset managers to offer environmentally and socially responsible investments to their clients. The asset managers, however, were not happy with this suggestion. They said the concept should be based on the actual demand of the clients, which was something to which the analysts did not have direct access. After a long discussion, the analysts and the asset managers agreed to jointly establish the new concept. The asset managers were responsible for identifying the clients' requirements, and the analysts were in charge of collecting data on responsible investing as a trend and of providing asset managers with an overall narrative for the concept.

This division of labor shows that the cooperation between asset managers and analysts is based on the fact that, in the creation of investment strategies, the two groups claim to have expertise in different fields. Although the asset managers acknowledge that analysts are valuable actors in producing background research and narratives, they claim that analysts do not know what clients really want. Analysts, in turn, argue that they should be the only ones that develop investment strategies, since asset managers do not have the necessary analytical skills to understand how markets develop over time. Thus, analysts usually complained about the asset managers who wanted to be involved in setting up investment strategies. As Marco suggested, the analysts' complaint was linked to what he called the "individualistic culture" at Swiss Bank. On various occasions, Marco explained that Swiss Bank's analysts in Singapore and Dubai have much more authority:

> In Singapore, Kim [Swiss Bank's head of analysis in Singapore] tells asset managers and client advisers exactly how they should invest. Kim and her team develop a strategy and all the managers and advisers follow her advice. It's not like here, where the asset managers and client advisers all think that they know how best to invest and that it's not important to listen to us.

Marco's statement indicates that financial analysts, after having established an investment narrative, try to gain influence in the investment process. Their efforts create tension between themselves and asset managers, because the asset managers also interpret markets. Here, the importance of market interpretation as being something unique and individual leads to an competitive relationship between analysts and asset managers. On the one hand, asset managers benefit from the analysts' investment narratives, which they can pass on as expert knowledge to clients. On the other hand, they want to create their own analyses to gain a sense of agency that allows them to think of their activity as not relying entirely on analysts.

The Politics of Narratives in Client Advice

The relationship between financial analysts and client advisers, who are responsible for giving investment advice to individual clients, is different from the relationship between analysts, asset managers, and institutional clients. Institutional clients are professionals themselves; they manage other people's funds professionally. Individual clients, on the other hand, manage their own money and often do not have the time and expertise necessary for studying market developments and gathering information. Therefore, to them, the narrative constructed by the analysts often is more important and less frequently challenged by other narratives. With individual clients financial analysts can perform their role as experts and can claim that their forecasts are fully reliable. In order to do so, however, they have to find ways of transmitting their knowledge via client advisers, who are the official points of contact with individual clients.

Financial analysts sometimes complain that client advisers are unsophisticated actors who do not understand markets and the importance of the financial analysts' predictions. In order to reach individual clients, however, analysts have to learn to deal with client advisers. The financial analysts' investment reports are distributed to client advisers, who then discuss them with the bank's clients. The analysts' antagonistic view of the client advisers thus partly stems from the fact that client advisers are in charge of passing on their narratives to the bank's clients, which is a process over which analysts have little control.

Talking with client advisers about the clients' attitudes toward analysts, I found that it varies substantially. Many clients believe in the expertise of financial analysts, others do not take any account of their views at all. Many of the analysts felt uncomfortable knowing that clients deal with their investment recommendations in very individualistic ways. When I asked analysts about their perception of clients, I found that "the client" is mostly used as an abstract concept in the financial analysis department. When discussing the effect of investment narratives, analysts often asked each other whether a story could be understood by the client. Once, when I was asking them about their actual idea of who the client is, one analyst said that he thinks of his mother or grandmother as being the client and then checks whether his story is something that his mother or grandmother could understand.

In fact, analysts know very little about the clients who are the ultimate recipients of their investment recommendations. There are two explanations for this. First, for privacy reasons, client advisers are reluctant to share any information about their clients with other parties, including financial analysts. Second, as in the case of the asset managers, many of the client advisers do not want to be too closely tied to the analysts' perspective. They want to develop their own investment strategies and establish a relationship with the client that is not undermined by the expert opinion of analysts.

As I learned when talking with client advisers, some clients have their own investment philosophy that does not necessarily coincide with the investment narratives the analysts provide. Consequently, they prefer to stick to their own approach instead of accepting the analysts' views. Other clients are aware of financial analysts' reports and read them but do not take them into account in their investment strategy. Some clients have had bad experiences with analyst recommendations in the past. Others simply do not believe in analysts' expertise, or they think that the financial analysts do not construct their market forecasts to help individual clients, but rather to promote particular stocks in which the bank itself has a business interest.

During my stay at Swiss Bank's Dubai office, I got to meet two young German investors. Both of them were active in day trading, an investment style in which traders buy and sell large numbers of stocks in a very short time in order to benefit from minimal volatility in the markets. Talking to these two investors, who had moved from Germany to Dubai to save taxes, I learned that they had their own unique perspective on the work of financial analysts. Their theory was that, instead of giving well-intentioned advice, the bank uses the analysts to engage in a kind of zero-sum game with its clients. In this scenario, the bank's management tells its analysts to advise clients to sell a particular stock, for example. If many clients follow the advice, the stocks will lose value. At the end of the day, the bank itself then buys the stocks at a premium. After the bank has bought the stock at a low price, it will become apparent that the stock price has fallen for no legitimate reason and investors will start buying the stocks again over the following weeks. The bank thus benefits from the rising stock prices, for it already owns the stocks that the investors are buying.

The young German day traders thus argued that banks hire in-house analysts to trick their own clients. To benefit from this, they told me, they themselves often buy the stocks that in-house analysts recommend selling, and sell the stocks that analysts recommend buying—a strategy that is sometimes called contrarian investing (see Hansen 2015). Of course, the German day traders' theory is merely another way of trying to understand how markets work. Although many investors probably do not share their view, their story still provides an interesting insight into their way of making sense of market developments. Also, the German day traders' theory does not oppose the notion that financial analysts are influential actors. Even though the German day traders argued that financial analysts work in favor of their host institutions and not for the bank's clients, they still gave credit to the fact that the forecasts and interpretations of financial analysts matter.

Selling a Story to a Client

The story of the German day traders is one example of a group of individual clients who do not accept the investment narratives of financial analysts as a simple guideline for investing. The general feedback on reports and forecasts, however, suggest it is fair to assume that a majority of clients perceive financial analysts' opinions as sophisticated investment advice. Individual clients with less access to alternative market views generally rely on the views of financial analysts. For the financial analysts, it is thus of crucial importance that they are able to circulate their opinions on market developments between wealth managers and clients. I mentioned before that financial analysts do not often meet clients in person. At Swiss Bank, analysts must communicate their views to client advisers and asset managers, who then pass these views on to the clients. This process has been designed to reduce possible conflicts between the analysts' market views and the wealth managers' duty to maximize the clients' financial benefit while taking account of their risk preferences.

Although a large part of selling a story to the client is via investment reports, analysts occasionally have the opportunity to engage personally with a client. This happens if wealth managers ask analysts to attend a meeting or participate in a telephone call to explain their view. Such opportunities are usually very important to analysts because they can use them to reinforce their influence by promoting their story directly. As a new member of the analyst community, I never had the chance to attend such a meeting. Swiss Bank's management allows only a few senior analysts to talk with clients because so much is at stake. After the meetings or telephone calls, however, the senior analysts sometimes talked with me and the junior analysts and shared their thoughts on the meeting and whether they felt that they had succeeded in convincing the client of their investment narrative.

Tobias, for example, once described a meeting he had with a group of clients in a Swiss country club. He is an excellent storyteller and therefore was asked to talk to a group of clients at an event organized by the bank. He told me that his talk about current market developments was just a small part of the broader program of the event. Before he gave his talk, a local winegrower had talked about the production of Swiss wine. The atmosphere was relaxed, and the audience, predominantly consisting of elderly male clients, were smoking cigars and waiting for Tobias to present his latest impressions on the market.

Tobias went to the event well prepared, bringing along a presentation of about thirty slides, packed with charts indicating the latest facts and figures on the state of the financial markets. He found, however, that the clients were not interested in detailed data. They wanted to discuss more general perspectives on the market. Back in the office, the more experienced members of the analysts' group discussed how Tobias should have approached these clients. One member of the management told Tobias that, rather than focusing on data, charts, and figures, it is important to use concepts with which clients are familiar, but to still be able to tell them something they did not already know. In such situations, analysts face the difficult task of navigating between narratives, concepts, and images that are familiar to the clients and the presentation of complex material that reinforces their status as experts. They often address the task by beginning with an overall concept that is easy to understand and then going into more complex issues to show they have special expertise that helps them to predict market movements.

At Swiss Bank, one concept that was frequently used to convince clients to invest in a particular future scenario was called Macro Growth.[1] Macro Growth was first introduced in the 1980s in social sciences as an analytic means of categorizing long-term epochal trends that had a transformative character for society as a whole. Unlike short-term trends, Macro Growth was understood as a bundle of macro-structural transformations that cannot be categorized as being either economic, political, social, or cultural, but rather embraces all these dimensions at once. To use anthropological language, they are thus seen as total social facts (Mauss [1923] 2002). Closely linked to the emerging discourse on globalization during the 1980s, Macro Growth aimed to explain macro-structural shifts that affected both people and economies on a global scale.

The concept of Macro Growth quickly became redundant in the social sciences, but it experienced a revival in finance more than two decades later. The reason for the revival may have been the persuasiveness of millennial discourse, in which the start of the new millennium encouraged many experts to think and talk about the longer-term future of the economy and society (see Comaroff and Comaroff 2000). To financial analysts, the revival was certainly also due to the concept's ability to bundle various transformations into one concept that seemed to grasp all the important transformations of the late twentieth and early twenty-first century.

When it came to establishing and promoting Macro Growth, the accuracy of the predictions was not as important as having a concept that could make sense of trends such as the future of a globalized economy, the shortage of resources, and the emergence of new digital technologies. Unlike a classical investment narrative, Macro Growth provided a framework that could unify multiple investment narratives. Moreover, Macro Growth was heavily influenced by the demands of asset managers and client advisers, who helped construct Swiss Banks's version of the concept as something that was marketable to their clients. Although the construction of investment narratives thus remained the domain of the analysts, Macro Growth offered a way of reinforcing the single narratives by bundling them in a concept that was designed to meet the demands of Swiss Bank's clients.

In 2010 Swiss Bank and a number of other financial institutions launched a series of investment products that claimed to take financial advantage of the transformations described in the concept of Macro Growth. The storyline was persuasive: The globalized world is experiencing a number of structural shifts that will fundamentally transform economics, politics, and society in the long run. By betting on these shifts, investors are likely to benefit from the long-term growth of particular sectors and companies that are prepared to provide the material needs and services that will be favored as these new trends emerge. Put this way, Macro Growth provided all the Swiss Bank employees who were involved in developing investment strategies with an attractive supernarrative, which could be linked to the investment narratives and decisions.

Loosely building on the 1980s scientific concept of Macro Growth, Swiss Bank felt free to redefine the components of the original concept to suit their own vision of the future. The negotiations on what should be considered as a macro-structural transformation started about two years before the launch of the first financial product and continued during the time I was with Swiss Bank. Inspired by the original concept, Swiss Bank defined its own thematic clusters of transformations. For each cluster, they then identified a number of investment themes, which were economic sectors and fields that they felt *supported* and *were supported by* the emergence of a particular macro-structural transformation.

Of course, Swiss Bank's analysts did not simply seek to identify clusters of macro-structural transformations. They primarily looked for transformations that could be financially exploited. For each cluster, analysts tried to think of companies that already existed and that could financially benefit from emerging trends. Some of the investment themes were easy to link to investments; with others it took a considerable amount of research to find out which companies and market sectors might benefit.

One cluster focused on sustainability as a macro-structural transformation. In that case, analysts primarily focused on companies that were active in developing technical infrastructure for using solar energy and hydropower. They also favored companies that were active in the privatization of water, arguing that the trend toward a more conscious use of water meant companies that own water would become more powerful. This, however, was in conflict with another cluster, which was called community. For this cluster, analysts claimed that companies that paid attention to the well-being of communities would benefit from long-term structural transformations.

As part of Swiss Bank's analysis team, I was involved in several discussions on conflicting strategies of this type. I discovered that some of the analysts thought there was no conflict in recommending stocks of companies that privatize and in companies that care about the community. They explained that the privatization of water was not something that they considered to be harmful per se. Putting a price on water, they argued, only made water more appreciated by the people consuming it. Challenging the view that the recommendations were in conflict, they usually repeated an argument that people like Peter Brabeck, former CEO and current chairman of Nestlé, have long used to justify companies' activities in privatizing water: governments should provide citizens in need with a certain amount of water, while the rest of the water is sold by companies in a free-market environment. A market for water makes it possible to put a price on resources, which is generally considered to be a good thing by most financial analysts.

A similar line of argumentation dominated other recommendations in the communities cluster. To benefit financially from the transformation to a greater focus on the well-being of communities, analysts advised clients to invest in microfinance institutions to enable poor people to set up entrepreneurial projects.[2] Inside the financial analysis department microfinance was by no means an uncontroversial topic. In fact, some of the financial analysts harshly criticized microfinance for being an exploitative instrument. Marco, a senior analyst, even told me that he thought microfinance, in its current form, should be forbidden: "Do you know how much interest they charge? Up to 50 percent! That's not interest, it's usury. They would never allow it in Switzerland."

In order to sell the Macro Growth storyline and because they knew that microfinance was popular among clients, however, the financial analysts did not integrate any of this criticism into their investment reports and client briefings. Moreover, the analysts who did not share the critical view of microfinance would repeat, like a mantra, Milton Friedman's quote that "the poor stay poor not because they are lazy but because they have no access to capital."[3] The logic here was the same as for the privatization of water: Markets that are accessible to all create equal opportunities and equal obligations for everyone.

For the analysts to recommend a company's stock as a part of the Macro Growth framework, the company had to be in line with the overall concept and be valuated positively in terms of its financial standing. In this respect, the case of education, which formed another cluster in the Macro Growth concept, represented a serious issue. During one of the meetings I attended, the cluster education was discussed in detail. The issue was that, even though most of the financial analysts thought that education was an attractive sector in which to invest, the transnational and publically listed companies active in that sector did not perform well. Some of the analysts argued that long-term growth did not always align with short-term success, but others felt that it would be dangerous to recommend stocks that were not currently performing well. Soon the discussion developed into a broader debate about whether long-term growth matters to investors at all or whether Macro Growth is simply a marketing trick to sell the analysts' investment narratives.

Large investment concepts like Macro Growth show how investment narratives—indirectly or directly—circulate between clients and analysts. They are successful when linked to a storyline that is understandable to all clients. But to wealth managers, such concepts also must reaffirm the current developments of stock prices. A good narrative without good performance is not enough. Neither, however, is good performance without a good narrative. Still, the concept of Macro Growth did sometimes manage to link good performance to good narratives. For that reason the concept became successful among the representatives of Swiss Bank.

"Shoot All the Analysts":
The Importance of Externalizing Failure

Supernarratives such as Macro Growth create an opportunity to harmonize the interests of financial analysts and wealth managers. At Swiss Bank, however, efforts to turn all investment views into supernarratives were opposed anyway. The reason was that the division of labor—in which analysts create narratives while asset wealth managers choose whether to use, amend, or ignore them—creates an important advantage. If an investment decision results in a loss, the actors involved benefit from the fact that the division of labor diffuses responsibility. In contact with clients, wealth managers can blame the analysts for having provided them with a loss-making investment narrative. Financial analysts, on the other hand, can blame the wealth managers for having executed the investment recommendation in a way that was not originally intended by the analysts.[4]

The relationship between analysts and wealth managers is thus characterized by an interplay between proximity and distance. When analysts and wealth managers create proximity, they can streamline their perspectives on market movements and create a supernarrative that is persuasive and marketable. When they create distance, they can reject claims of being responsible for certain predictions and investment decisions by externalizing failure to the other group of market participants involved.

In March 2001 the *Financial Times* published the editorial "Shoot

All the Analysts." As a reaction to the dotcom bubble, a growing number of financial market participants and journalists started to blame financial analysts for the huge losses on the stock markets after the bubble had burst. Financial analysts, the article argued, "should learn a little humility and get back to analysis." Even though the *Financial Times* significantly contributed to the successful establishment of analysts as market experts by giving them a voice before the bubble burst, it clearly expressed its disappointment in the negative development of stock prices around that time. Instead of blaming structural developments or management failure, the paper blamed financial analysts for the losses. Of course, the *Financial Times* had good reason to blame the analysts, because many financial forecasts around that time turned out to be terribly wrong. Also, as revealed in the editorial and elsewhere, a lot of financial analysts had personal financial incentives to make companies look better than they actually were (Dreman 2002; "Shoot All" 2001).

The treatment analysts received around 2001 shows how convenient it can be to have a group of actors who can be blamed by the other market participants if something unexpected happens in the markets. At Swiss Bank, I sometimes experienced such externalization of responsibility by wealth managers. When a wrong prediction created a substantial loss on a client's portfolio, analysts often served as scapegoats. Sometimes, asset managers or client advisers then contacted an analyst to complain. In these situations, analysts knew exactly how to react. They remained calm and would usually explain to the wealth managers about this or that event that could not have been predicted.

Unexpected events arise regularly: floods, political uprisings, or an unexpected fall in interest rates. When such events occur, analysts often change their recommendations early in the morning and tell the wealth managers that the error in forecasting has already been corrected. To my surprise, however, these telephone calls were rather rare in comparison with the amount of investment advice analysts gave and how often they turned out to be wrong. Talking to various wealth managers, I realized that, instead of communicating their displeasure to the analysts, many of them simply used these undesirable developments to appease their clients by blaming bad financial results on the financial analysts.

Blaming analysts is clearly a convenient strategy for wealth managers if one of their investments takes a loss. Ultimately, however, they also know that the financial analyst is not the only party at fault. Talking to wealth managers, I found that very few of them simply took the recommendations of analysts when choosing their investment strategies. As I mentioned earlier, the investment narratives provided by analysts are just one reference point in their decision-making process. They also have their own beliefs on how markets might develop and, most important, they have to take into account how their clients wish to invest their money. Various sources influence the way they choose to invest their money, and wealth managers experience success and failure in predicting market movements just as analysts do. In personal talks about the establishment of their investment strategy, they thus usually stressed that failure cannot actually be blamed on financial analysts alone, for they reflect on the recommendations of analysts and can ignore them if they like. Blaming analysts for loss-making decisions is thus many times a way of externalizing responsibility after the fact, rather than an expression of truly having been misguided by financial analysts.

Situations in which wealth managers directly contacted analysts to blame them for their loss-making decisions were thus relatively rare. Whenever it happened, however, it revealed something interesting. These interactions with wealth managers created a situation in which analysts were forced to reflect on the financial effects of their investment recommendations. When analysts talk about the influence of their investment recommendations, they usually focus on how many managers and clients like their ideas and how many clients asked to read the full investment report. The actual economic performance of the analysts' forecasts, though, are rarely ever actively discussed. In general, discussion of the analysts' forecasts is not only avoided but even actively suppressed. It seems to be an unwritten rule that analysts do not ask other analysts about their past forecasts or check their performance. The reason for this convention is clear: Looking at the actual performance of past forecasts, one can easily see that analysts often fail to correctly forecast market developments.

This "don't ask, don't tell" approach among analysts was challenged in 2011, when Eva became the head of all financial market research teams after a restructuring of the financial analysis department. Coming from fixed-income research, Eva did not take into account the stock market analysts' habit of not talking about the performance of past forecasts. And, as a reaction to the ongoing crisis, every department in Swiss Bank was forced to increase its accountability and report to the top management about their cost effectiveness (see Strathern 2000). Hence, Eva thought that introducing a performance measurement of forecasts would be a good way of showing the management how costs are transferred into benefits through the work of financial analysts.

The analysts hated Eva's idea. Soon after Eva had announced that she wanted to start measuring the performance of forecasts, the analysts started to challenge any possible method that could be used for such a measurement. Chris told me that to measure the quality of a forecast, one cannot simply compare it to the overall market development. Instead, one has to compare the prediction to some kind of benchmark to measure the performance relative to the performance of other stocks from companies with similar size, strategy, and business focus. "For many forecasts, however," Chris claimed, "there is no such valid benchmark. You can end up being lucky and the benchmark companies perform badly or you can be unlucky and the benchmark companies outperform your forecast. In both cases, there can never be a fair measurement." As a consequence, Chris tried to sabotage the performance measures that Eva and the top management aimed to implement by relativizing their validity in personal discussions with other analysts.

Many of the financial analysts shared Chris's opinion and tried to convince Eva that measuring the performance of past forecasts could not be done accurately. Suddenly, the professional measurers became critical of any measurement practices. Eva, however, was not fazed by the analysts' criticisms. About three months after her announcement, a system of performance measurements was introduced. Starting from then, all stock market analysts received a monthly report on everyone's forecasting performance. It became clear that many of the forecasts of well-experienced and renowned analysts were in fact less accurate than some of the forecasts of junior analysts. The reaction to the report was mixed. Individual analysts sometimes criticized the measurement techniques and the benchmarking (mostly after having received a bad performance result), most of the time they just chose not to talk about the results. The measurements were obviously never mentioned in communications with wealth managers. Rather than measuring the past, the financial analysts kept focusing on constructing narratives about the future.

As this shows, through mechanisms that disseminate responsibility, financial analysts sometimes externalize failure. At other times, they strategically disregard it. When I spoke to the analysts in person, however, many had a bad feeling about disregarding the actual performance of past recommendations. This was partly because it challenged the legitimacy of their profession and partly because, after 2008, financial analysts were facing an unprecedented situation. Prior to this crisis, markets generally increased in value in the long run. Some forecasts thus might have been loss-making in the short term, but since overall market prices increased over time, clients were usually happy when they benefited from the market growth. If a crisis occurred, as it did in the Swiss housing market in the 1990s for example, it made the analysts look bad. Prior to 2008, however, such crises usually did not last for very long, and when the clients realized that something had gone wrong, analysts could advise them to invest in alternative markets that were not affected by a particular crisis.

After 2008, however, the situation was different. The crisis was long, it was global, and alternative investment opportunities were hard to find. Although they still claimed to be able to see investment opportunities, analysts admitted to me that they sometimes had no idea where the crisis would take the market. The additional externalization of failure from wealth managers only reinforced their insecurity and guilt. Paul, an analyst responsible for companies working in the extractive industry, once started a conversion during lunchtime about this particular feeling. In a partly ironic, partly desperate voice, he said, "You know, all the people out there want to know who is responsible for the crisis. I am telling you: it's us! We recommended buying all this bullshit, these risky stocks, and these structured products. They don't even know, but it's us."

Analysts as Animators

In his presidential address to the American Finance Association in 2008, Kenneth French (2008, 1558) described the role of market intermediaries such as analysts as being based on a "futile search for superior returns" that costs investors an average of 0.67 percent of their returns per year in comparison with passive investment strategies. Since the rise of financial markets, active investing—that is, investing based on expert recommendations and asset management strategies—has indeed become a multi-billion-dollar industry. Bogle (2008, 97) estimates that the United States spent US$528 billion on financial services for active investment in 2007 alone (which is about 4 percent of the country's GDP; see Marti and Scherer 2016). This large sum is all the more surprising if one considers that active investing goes against the core assumption of market efficiency. It evokes the paradox noted at the beginning of this book: that financial analysis exists as a practical field despite the fact that its practices are fiercely challenged by neoclassical economics and empirical findings.

Financial analysts are promoters of active investment. They manage to take on this role by building a strong symbiotic relationship to the wealth manager, their host institution (Swiss Bank, in my case) and the public. In all these relationships, it becomes apparent that analysts not only offer investment narratives for interested recipients but actively *animate* investors to buy or sell stocks and other financial products. Host institutions have a large interest in analysts being animators, for they usually earn commission every time an investor buys or sells a financial product. Investors, even though they might be aggrieved by the work of analysts, accept the role of analysts as animators, because it gives them a sense of agency. Instead of having to merely observe market movements and likewise the development of their wealth, *being animated* by analysts allows investors to think of themselves as active players who can make decisions and thus influence the development of their wealth in the market.

The Corporate Role of Analysts

The relationship between financial analysts and Swiss Bank as their host institution is intriguing and sometimes prone to conflict. Officially, many representatives of the bank describe the role of analysts as a straightforward service to the bank's clients. As service providers, financial analysts are presented as independent market experts by the bank as well as by the Swiss financial regulatory authority FINMA. In a statement of 2008, FINMA (2008, 4) defines the role of financial analysts by referring to the Swiss Bankers Association's *Directives on the Independence of Financial Research* (2008), which is a code of conduct for financial analysts drawn up by the financial services industry itself.[1] In the directives, the Swiss Bankers Association highlights three domains in which active measures need to be implemented in order to ensure the independence of the work of analysts.

The first domain regulates the intraorganizational independence of financial analysts. The document states that "The organizational unit responsible for financial research [. . .] must be independent, from an organizational, hierarchical, functional and locational perspective, from the unit that is responsible for issuing securities and for investment banking" (Swiss Bankers Association 2008, 5). The same intraorganizational independence is expected from "securities trading (including proprietary trading) and sales" (7) and from "any units responsible for lending business" (9).

The second domain addresses the role of remuneration. The Swiss Bankers Association states that "The remuneration paid to financial analysts must not be dependent upon the performance (revenues or performance targets) of one or more specific transaction(s) of the new issues department of investment banking" (Swiss Bankers Association 2008, 5). Similarly, it specifies that remuneration must not depend on the performance of transactions done in the bank's securities trading department (7).

For the third domain, the directives give instructions on how to avoid informational asymmetries within the organization itself. The Swiss Bankers Association states that "The new issues department and investment banking operations of a bank and its financial research unit must be structured in such manner that basically no privileged information ('material, non-public' information) flows between them that is not simultaneously available to clients of the bank (Chinese walls)"[2] (Swiss Bankers Association 2008, 6). Similarly, a number of paragraphs focus on so-called front running (6–8). Front running is a prohibited market practice in which nonpublic information is strategically obtained or employed for speculative purposes.

All three of these domains address the relationship between financial market knowledge and financial market practices. They aim to prevent practices that are based on privileged access to knowledge. By regulating informational flows between analysts and other actors with privileged access to information, the code makes sure that information is spread equally among all market participants.[3]

At Swiss Bank, the code of conduct published by the Swiss Bankers Association is known and incorporated into the setup of the financial analysis department within the bank. As required by the guidelines, financial analysts operate independently from the investment banking unit and the trading units of the bank. Also, there are no direct incentives for the Swiss Bank analysts to adjust their investment advice to the trading strategy of the bank or to support the bank's new offering of stocks from an analytical point of view.

The implementation of the code of conduct in everyday workflows does not, however, mean that Swiss Bank treats the financial analysis department as an entirely independent services unit. To the bank, financial analysts are responsible for encouraging clients to invest. Chris once made this very clear when we were talking about the corporate role of financial analysts. He pointed out that even during the worst period of the financial crisis, the head of the financial analysis team encouraged analysts to keep on looking for "strong calls," that is, investment recommendations that indicate opportunities to generate profit by buying particular stocks. Clearly, banks such as Swiss Bank have a financial interest in having their clients investing actively in markets, because clients pay fees every time they buy or sell a stock. Clients try to get a maximum financial return, and the bank tries to maximize a client's turnover rate in the portfolio. To achieve this, banks rely on financial analysts who continuously create, amend, and reformulate investment advice so that clients keep buying and selling financial products, even if they would be better off not doing so.

The motivation of a host bank to have financial analysts who continuously create narratives that promote the buying and selling of products is sometimes in conflict with the clients' interests in achieving maximum financial returns. Therefore, host banks indirectly ensure that analysts act in their interests. By providing analysts with lucrative employment, they create economic incentives for the analysts to enact the host bank's interests.

Responding to a number of extremely bad forecasts and scandals in the aftermath of the dotcom bubble, David Dreman (2002), a renowned asset manager, raised this particular problem in an editorial commentary published in the *Journal of Psychology and Financial Markets*. Referring to various surveys and observations, Dreman notes that the level of analysts' bonuses is not influenced by the accuracy of their forecasts, but primarily by their ability to make investors buy stocks (138). To Dreman, this indicates that financial analysts are not the independent market experts they try to impersonate. Their desire for large bonuses means that their interests are aligned with the host corporation's interests.

During my time with Swiss Bank, however, I found that the story is not quite as simple as that. Although Dreman criticizes the fact that analysts do not get paid according to the accuracy of their predictions, the Swiss Bankers Association sees the decoupling of remuneration and accuracy of forecasts as a way of preventing individual analysts from working with insider information. Generally, there is a thin line between the role of the analyst as independent expert and the analyst as actor on behalf of his or her host institution. When I spoke to nonanalyst financial market participants about my research, some of them told me that they generally presume that analysts prefer to recommend stocks in which their host institution has a business interest (a point I mentioned in the example of the German day traders in chapter 7). My experience during fieldwork, however, showed that such was not the case.

Financial analysis, at least on the buy side, is strongly regulated and supervised. The analysts at Swiss Bank, to my knowledge, rarely have any information about whether the bank has a future business interest in a particular company they are covering. If the bank has a current business interest in a particular company, the stocks count as restricted for financial analysts. This means that analysts are not permitted to make any recommendation or give their perspective on the particular stock to clients. These restrictions are widely accepted by the management of Swiss Bank and the analysts. The influence of the host institution on the analysts' calls is thus not straightforward, but structural.

What do I mean by structural influence? During my time with the analysts, I saw that they had a strong preference for issuing buy ratings and were cautious about advising clients to sell particular stocks. Although there was no official rule on the relation between buy, hold, and sell recommendations, many analysts told me that they think at least 50 percent of all stock market ratings should be buy-rated. They said that most of the other 50 percent should be hold-rated, and that sell ratings should never exceed 20 to 25 percent. Maintaining that split was not always easy, particularly during one of the many difficult phases I experienced, when the entire stock market was clearly losing value. In these cases, analysts argued that most of the companies would recover in the long run and that they would not want to change their rating to a sell recommendation because clients would not benefit in the long run if they missed the opportunity to buy the stocks again before they rise. As independent market observers, they should have at least been able to recommend selling 100 percent of the stocks if they felt that the markets were going down, and then return to a buy recommendation only when they felt that the stock value was about to increase again.

Analysts, however, preferred to stay bullish (telling investors to buy stocks). Discussing this bias during lunch with the analysts, they told me that they have strong reservations about any signal of disinvesting. Disinvesting, they argued, is bad for the economy. They see their job as looking for the upside opportunities, no matter how bad the general market outlook is. This optimism, as a frame, existed among all analysts when constructing their investment narratives.

Sometimes, this optimistic bias led to tricky situations. In the first half of 2011, for example, Richard, the head of the financial analysis department, continuously advised investors to buy stocks. After stock prices had risen for almost a year, Richard interpreted this development as an ongoing trend. In August 2011, however, turbulence in the Eurozone and the reemergence of concerns about the stability of the banking sector triggered the start of the "big sell-off," as analysts called it. In less than three months, the MSCI World Index lost a third of its market value. Nevertheless, Richard's instruction to buy stocks, despite being disastrous to some investors, was not a hotly debated topic within the financial analysis department. Some of the analysts who did not like Richard for personal or professional reasons complained about the situation, calling Richard incompetent. His optimistic bias, though, which was echoed in the narratives of most of the other analysts, was rarely subject to discussion.[4]

Another indirect influence that the business interests of Swiss Bank have on the everyday work of financial analysts concerns the frequency of changing one's investment strategy. I mentioned before that banks have a financial interest in encouraging clients to change their strategy once in a while to generate fees from buying and selling. Of course, Swiss Bank cannot urge analysts to change their recommendation solely for the purpose of generating fees. Still, the bank's interest of benefiting from ever-changing investment advice has synergies with the analysts' aim of producing a large number of investment reports that present them as active respondents to market movements.

Although most analysts were quite skeptical about using the accuracy of forecasts as a measure of quality, the frequency of publishing new or adjusted investment strategies was widely accepted as a valid measure of an analyst's performance. When measuring the performance of analysts, the heads of the various analyst teams almost always considered the publishing frequency of their team members.

Andy, for example, was a member of the analysis department who chose to switch to another banking unit after having spent about four years in the financial analysis department. During his farewell party, which took place at Swiss Bank's in-house bar, Marco, his former boss, gave a speech to celebrate Andy's achievements. To stress the value of Andy as an analyst, Marco read out some statistics to the other employees who had come to have a drink and wish Andy farewell. "Last year," Marco proudly stated, "Andy published fifty-two investment reports. That is more than anyone else in the financial analysis department." The number impressed the listeners. They showed their reaction by turning to each other and nodding in an approving manner. After Marco's speech, the analysts discussed the large number of reports that Andy had written. Everyone seemed to agree that the frequency of publishing new investment reports was a legitimate measure of Andy's performance.

Hence, encouraging clients to read investment reports and engage in ever-changing investment activities is a goal that both the bank and the analysts share. They create an environment in which clients are continuously animated to adjust their investment strategies. The message is clear: A good investment today is not necessarily a good investment tomorrow. Of course, analysts cannot change the ratings of single stocks every week. Therefore, much of the investment encouragement is done by either creating new thematic investment topics or responding to current trends. I exemplified this earlier by looking at the instrumentalization of events such as the Arab Spring, or trends such as the moralization of market behavior for investment purposes. Integrating these trends and events into financial analysis is a way of continually creating new investment strategies that generate fees for the bank and make the analysts look like indispensable market participants. Both the bank and its analysts thus benefit from changing environments, volatile markets, and even from economic and political crises, for these situations allow them to create new narratives that are communicated as opportunities to invest to their clients.

Analysts and Their External Relationships

Like the regulatory directives designed to prevent conflicts of interest between analysts and their host institution, the Swiss Bankers Association (2008) gives advice on how the relationship between analysts and clients should be organized in order to avoid conflicts. In its directives, the association highlights three domains of regulation of analysts and those outside the institutions for whom they work.

First, as with the directives on the internal flows of information, the Swiss Bankers Association advises banks to make sure that no asymmetrical flows of information take place between analysts and external parties. This concerns asymmetrical flows of information about a company to be valuated to both the analysts and the recipients of the investments reports. In terms of the information flows from companies to analysts, the directive states the following:

> As a rule, a company shall not disclose to individual analysts any kind of privileged ("material, non-public") information. If an analyst nevertheless does receive privileged information in the course of his/her activity, he/she shall decide in consultation with the Compliance unit on how to proceed, in particular, on whether to refrain from publishing the report or recommendation, as well as on whether to disclose the fact that the information could have been privileged. (Swiss Bankers Association 2008, 12)

Regarding market knowledge provided to clients, it states that "As a rule, reports and recommendations by financial analysts, particularly any ratings that are published or changed, are to be made available to all recipients in a client category (recipient group) within and outside the bank at the same time. Internal and external parties and offices may only be given advance notice in exceptional cases and in accordance with the Directives of the Compliance unit" (Swiss Bankers Association 2008, 11).

Second, the role of legal disclosures is highlighted and regulated: "In any published research report, the bank must disclose whether it has participated in the last 12 months in any issue of securities on behalf of the company being researched" (Swiss Bankers Association 2008, 7). Additional rules on disclosing information are mentioned in the case of analysts who receive remuneration or privileged information from a company, something that in fact breaches the Swiss Bankers Association's guidelines. By disclosing such possible conflicts of interests, the directive states, the analysts can redeem themselves (5–10).

The third domain sets out standards for the analysts' independence in terms of the company to be valuated and for their integrity as people who are not aiming to take advantage of the investment recommendations themselves. The directive states that "A financial analyst may not accept any privileges, gifts or any other [favors] from the company being analyzed where the value of such privileges, gifts or [favors exceeds] that of normal occasional gifts. If there is any doubt, the analyst must notify the Compliance Unit about any offers received" (Swiss Bankers Association 2008, 14). In terms of the analysts' integrity, the rules are as follows: "A financial analyst may not acquire for his/her own account any securities which he/she researches (securities, uncertified securities, incl. derivatives)" (14). And "If an analyst holds an executive function, or has any other significant influence in the company to be researched, he/she may not prepare any research reports on the company" (15).

As far as I experienced it, flows of asymmetrical information were not exploited by analysts when analyzing companies. The relationship between companies to be valuated and the analysts are highly formalized. Analysts are careful to avoid building up friendly relationships with representatives of these companies so that they can critically valuate the companies' stock market performance. This effort on the part of analysts not to build up friendly ties with the companies to be valuated was astonishing to me. Such ties would have given analysts access to information that could have enabled them to make more accurate predictions. One probable reason they did not do so was that the analysts were not as keen on improving the accuracy of their market predictions as they were keen on producing high volumes of investment reports and good stories. Insider information did not really help in the short term, for it could not be integrated into the investment narrative. Therefore, analysts tend to prefer unconventional facts about a company (that probably do not influence the stock price much but help to establish a good story) over information that might influence the stock price but cannot be integrated into a narrative.

Manuel was one of the analysts who regularly met with representatives of companies he valuated. The meetings were usually organized by sell-side analysts, who were paid to offer such services to buy-side analysts. They took place either in one of Swiss Bank's meeting rooms or in a nearby hotel's conference room. Sometimes the company's representatives met with analysts from different banks at the same time, and sometimes the sell-analysts organized so-called one-on-ones, where the representatives met with one buy-side analyst alone. When I talked with Manuel about the meetings, he never mentioned the distribution of new market information in a strict sense. Rather, he explained he tried to find out whether he could trust the people involved in setting up a firm's strategy. "In these meetings, it's all about finding out whether a company has a true vision," said Manuel.

This focus on finding out about a company's vision and on developing faith in the people responsible for the company's strategy also became clear when looking at whom the companies usually sent to meet analysts. I rarely ever heard of meetings with a company's chief financial officer, who could have given the analysts the most accurate insights into the company's financial standing. Analysts rather met with the people responsible for marketing or the development of a strategy. The strength of these representatives was not an in-depth knowledge of a company's financial standing, but the ability to generate a narrative context of the development of the company they represented.

Manuel was particularly impressed after having met with a representative from a sports equipment manufacturer. After he returned from the meeting, he told the other analysts sitting near his desk about what had happened. He said that the company he had just met with studied the various perceptions of the company's brand in the United States and in Europe. It found that in the United States, the brand was perceived as a manufacturer of sports equipment, but in Europe, the company was perceived as a fashion label. Manuel thought this finding was exciting and very valuable. First, it was a piece of information that could eventually materialize in the market price, in that the company could use the study's result to improve its marketing. Second, and this was far more important to Manuel, it was an insight into the company that he could easily integrate into an investment narrative and pass on to the investors.

The example of Manuel being so excited about this insight exemplifies what analysts look for when meeting companies' representatives. Rather than looking for insider information, such as forthcoming numbers, mergers, and changes in strategies, they look for information that they can use in their investment reports to provide insights that are not based on the company's financial standing alone. In the company report analyzed in chapter 6, it became apparent that Marcel used a strategy of personalization to show recipients of his forecast that his investment story is not based simply on numbers and financial information. Similarly, Manuel appreciated most the information that allowed him to link financial information to an insight that could serve as the basis for a coherent narrative.

In contrast to the guidelines established by the Swiss Bankers Association that regulate the relationship between the analysts and com-

panies, the guidelines that prohibit analysts from investing in companies themselves were viewed from a much more critical perspective
by many of the analysts. I learned this when I first participated in the
regular briefing of analysts by the legal and compliance department.
Yang, the head of the legal and compliance team that was responsible
for controlling financial analysts, started her presentation in an easy-
going manner. She joked about the antagonistic relationship between
the analysts who always want the investors to follow their risky advice and the compliance officers who try to limit possible future dam-
age created by the risky advice. Yang reminded the analysts to think
about their clients, "especially the uneducated ones," and to try to
avoid persuading them to make investments that they did not understand. Also, she spoke a lot about the language they should be using:
"We don't want to see gambling-like language and expressions like
'play this stock' or 'bet on this company' in your investment reports."
In addition, she reminded the analysts that they cannot foresee the
future and thus should never use sentences like "the market will be
up five percent." Instead, they should write "we expect the market to
be up five percent."

The senior analysts that were present at the briefing had heard
these guidelines before. Many were thus sitting in the compulsory
meeting looking bored. Their demeanor changed, however, when
Yang brought up the topic of analysts investing in the market themselves. The directives of the Swiss Bankers Association forbid analysts
from investing in companies they analyze. In practice, however, this
directive is not so easy to implement. Many of the analysts cover a limited number of stocks themselves, but they also frequently collaborate
in broader thematic or regional reports, in which stocks covered by
other analysts also are mentioned. Situations can thus arise in which
a stock is mentioned in a report that was partly written by an analyst who holds the stock in his or her private portfolio. Rolling their
eyes, many of the analysts complained about what they considered
an unnecessary guideline. One analyst even told Yang that Swiss bank
secrecy meant that the legal and compliance department of Swiss
Bank would not even be able to check whether analysts hold the stocks
they analyze.

During that meeting, which took place after I had been in the field
for about three months, I initially thought the analysts were unhappy

about the guideline because it stopped them taking financial advantage of their own market knowledge and forecasts. Later, however, I discovered that their rejection of this particular guideline was for a different reason. The restriction on analysts participating in stock market investments prevents them from cultivating their affective connection to markets. To them, investing themselves meant that they could create spaces in which they could test expectations and bodily experience success and failure.

Marco, for example, was convinced that all analysts should invest in the stock market themselves. On several occasions, he, as well as other analysts, asked me whether I invested in the stock market myself. When I told them that I did not, some said it could be difficult for me to get a feeling of how markets work without having money invested myself. Andy usually mentioned his own investment activities when discussing his analyses. When he left the financial analysis department, one of his former colleagues gave a farewell speech in which he said that he very much appreciated that Andy was not an analyst who "hides behind his expertise," but rather was a hands-on guy who was not afraid "to put the money where his mouth is."

Analysts in Public Discourse

In addition to the frequency of publishing investment reports and the attention these reports earn among investors, an analyst's relevance also is defined by his or her ability to become part of public discourse. Swiss Bank's management encourages analysts to appear in the media, and the analysts themselves want to do so because it serves their aim of establishing legitimacy and influence. Being cited in a daily newspaper, for example, gives financial analysts the chance to bring their ideas to a wider public. To prepare for such appearances, financial analysts undertake training in how to talk to journalists. During these sessions, the analysts are briefed on how to bring across an investment narrative in different media and how to talk in front of a camera.

At Swiss Bank, a journalist from a local television station provided this training. This journalist was not a specialist in finance. On the contrary, his job was not to think about the content, but to teach financial analysts how appearance and gesture could influence the way experts are perceived by the audience when speaking on television. Also, the journalist focused on how to present complex content in a way the audience can easily understand. This training, organized by the management of Swiss Bank for the analysts in the format of a one-day workshop that took place once a year, was not mandatory. Most of the analysts, however, participated at least once to train their skills presenting themselves as experts to the public.

Some of the analysts liked being on television and in the newspapers, but others were not comfortable with the idea of presenting their market knowledge to a broader public. The management of the financial analysis department, however, made it very clear that it welcomed its analysts appearing in public. Those who were comfortable doing so actively promoted their success: After having appeared in the media, they usually sent around the newspaper article or the Internet link to the television show to prove that they had succeeded in becoming part of public discourse.

When talking to journalists, financial analysts usually are very careful to ensure that they present their market analysis in a way that fulfills the expectations of the newspaper's readership or the television station's viewers. Roughly speaking, financial analysts talk to three types of media: first, the media that specialize in financial markets (e.g., Bloomberg, the *Financial Times*, the *Wall Street Journal*, and their Swiss equivalents); second, the media (or media sections) that specialize in economics and business (e.g., the business sections of daily newspapers or television shows on economic issues); third, the unspecialized media (e.g., daily newspapers or general-interest television).

To target their audience, analysts adapt their narrative to suit the type of media in which it will appear. Talking to journalists from newspapers or television stations specialized in financial markets is the easiest task for financial analysts. They are free to use financial jargon. Because they are talking as experts to other experts, they try to underline their market knowledge by referring to calculative approaches, data sets, or recent studies on financial markets. Also, they sometimes make risky calls, because they know that their audience is made up of financial market professionals who are familiar with the risks of investing.

For media specialized in economic issues, financial analysts usually choose a different strategy for bringing across their investment narrative. Instead of using a line of argumentation and wording specific to financial markets, they try to translate their knowledge into a storyline that focuses on the economy as a whole. They highlight the significance of factors such as of long-term growth, the value of small and medium-sized enterprises, or the role of consumption. Looking at these differences in presentation style, it becomes apparent how financial analysts operate with different symbols and language. Analysts are experts in code switching, that is, playing with symbolic elements and switching vocabularies according to the audience they want to reach (Gumperz and Hymes 1986). This skill also is visible in the way analysts communicate with journalists who will be writing articles or producing content for media in the third category (unspecialized mainstream media). Here, experienced analysts reduce their expert language to a minimum and try to make statements that can be understood by anyone, regardless of whether they have any knowledge of how financial markets work.

Anne, who headed a team of about ten analysts and had a reputation for being very well connected, often talked to journalists from mainstream media. Her quotes and statements were very popular among journalists, because she was able to translate complex issues into a language that was easy to understand. Also, Anne had a very strong opinion on how financial market processes *should* be understood. Once, when I was talking to her about the relationship between economics and politics in Switzerland, she made this very clear: "You know, in finance, everything is logical: A leads to B, and that's a fact. But in politics, people just don't understand this logic." To her, economics represented a rational sphere, and other fields, such as politics, threaten its rationality. "I think that there should be many more economists in the government," she went on, sounding upset, "but in Berne [the home of Switzerland's parliament], you even find some people with a background in humanities in power."[5]

According to Anne, developments in markets always could be understood by relatively simple, logical reasoning. Her belief that everything that happened in the market could be understood in a relatively simple cause-and-effect analysis made Anne an attractive person for journalists from mainstream media to talk to. Instead of referring to complex calculative approaches or data sets, Anne had a knack for choosing very simple examples to explain complex issues. As if talking about mathematics, she would often refer to apples and pears to explain what different parties wanted to achieve and how they interacted. When asked about this reduction of complexity, Anne often said that what makes economics difficult is not economics itself, but the "irrationalities" introduced by "uneducated" investors and politicians. As she once told a journalist, understanding the market is easy, as long as you are not tricked by the "irrational ideologies of noneconomists who do not understand its straightforward logic."

One might assume that analysts want to appear as experts in specialized media but are not very keen on appearing in mainstream media. It is surprising, however, that at least for the senior analysts, it is often the other way around. Although giving interviews in the specialized media helps analysts to become known within the analyst community, being present in the mainstream media allows them to increase their influence even further. In the mainstream media, they often talk not only about single stocks and current performance, but about broader economic developments. In so doing, they can become part of a broader debate and reinforce their position as authoritative experts who are able to make sense of market movements.

Ironically, this became particularly apparent in the aftermath of the financial crisis. The failure of the financial market economy enabled many financial analysts to become part of a public debate on how to *overcome* a crisis. This was mainly because many people assumed that it was necessary to have much in-depth knowledge of financial markets to make suggestions on how to overcome the financial crisis (even though one could also have argued that it would be better to minimize the influence of financial market participants in these public debates).

Analysts like Anne were very happy to capitalize on this assumption. As a result, financial analysts managed to turn the financial crisis into an opportunity to increase their influence. They gave many television and newspaper interviews in which they explained why the crisis happened and presented possible ways of getting the markets "back on track." By responding to this public demand to have experts explaining crises, analysts could gain legitimacy in public while their legitimacy inside the market was being questioned. This again has to do with their ability to construct narratives. Surrounded by the uncertainty produced by the financial crisis, people started to look for storylines that explained how markets got into such a mess and how they could possibly get out of it. Financial analysts could provide narratives that seemed to make sense of the complex issues in a rather simple way and thus helped the public understand the crisis.[6]

To analysts, being part of public discourse is particularly important for three reasons: first, they can use their voice in public to make market developments look analytically explainable; second, they help to increase investment volume by continually animating investors, whether it be the bank's own clients or any investor following the media, to buy and sell financial products; third, by having a voice in public discourse, they reinforce processes of economization beyond the realm of financial markets.

Through their presence in the media, financial analysts reinforce the notion that financial markets are not a big casino (an accusation popularized by Susan Strange in her book *Casino Capitalism* in 1986 and repeated by many people during the crisis), but rather a field that can be scientifically analyzed. When talking to journalists, just as in their reports to the bank's clients, analysts try to represent financial market movements as events that can be rationally understood if the necessary information is available. In public discourse, financial analysts thus frame financial market operations in a way that ensures they do not appear as speculative and casino-like, but as a field that is governed by knowable "laws of the market" (see Callon 1998).

Second, through the construction of investment narratives, financial analysts help to increase overall market volume and the turnover rate of financial market products. In 1960 the average holding period for a stock listed on the New York Stock Exchange was eight years. This figure has fallen continuously during the last fifty years. In 2010 it was six months ("Stock Market Becomes Short Attention Span Theater" 2011; "Wisdom of Exercising Patience" 2012). Today, Chesney (2014) estimates that it is in the range of only a few minutes. This dramatic decline in the average holding time is partly due to the increasing volume of trades settled by high-frequency trading, which is trading using algorithmic programs that trade rapidly so as to exploit short time differences between price changes and, as such, benefit from volatile prices (see Lewis 2014; Pardo-Guerra 2012). The decline also, however, reflects the success of financial analysts, who constantly create new investment recommendations and animate investors to become active market participants.

In animating investors to become active, financial analysts also help to increase the total amount of money invested in financial markets. As I explained, analysts prefer to tell clients to buy stocks and hardly ever tell them to sell. Referring to various studies, Bruce (2002, 198) notes that, irrespective of the market situation, 50 percent of most analyst recommendations are buy recommendations, and less than 1 percent of investment advice recommends selling—a result that corresponds to the empirical observations I made in the field. Bruce says this bias is the result of analysts needing access to information about the companies they valuate. When analysts recommend selling a stock, the valuated company punishes them by stopping their access to information (Bruce 2002, 199; Dreman 2002, 139).

Among the buy-side analysts I studied, this is not the case, as they officially can only use publicly available data for their analyses anyway. With them, the tendency to recommend buying rather than selling stock does not reflect a motivation to getting access to data, but the way they think about markets in general. These analysts believe disinvesting hurts the overall economy and is thus morally problematic. As a consequence, they prefer to animate clients to buy stocks, even if the market outlook is in fact rather negative. On the structural level, this bias leads to an increasing number of total investments in the financial market.

A third effect of the presence of financial analysts in public discourse is linked to what is sometimes described as commodification.[7] To become tradable, things—material or immaterial—have to be measurable and priced. Analysts are such "economizers," to use an expression coined by Çalışkan and Callon (2009, 2010). They put a price tag on everything and, in so doing, they reinforce an economistic logic that suggests that everything, economic or noneconomic, can be made measurable and tradable.

In chapters 5 and 6, I elaborated on the processes of pricing noneconomic values when analysts talked about pricing in the corporate social responsibility of companies or the Egyptian revolution in 2011 (see also Leins 2011). Similar claims can be made for the period when Australia experienced devastating floods in 2011, after the nuclear catastrophe in Fukushima, when Mitt Romney was selected to run against Barack Obama, or when the NATO started military air strikes against Libya. Those events, which were not primarily understood as economic per se, motivated analysts to think about the events' economic impact and to translate environmental, political, and social aspects into market signals.

In so doing, financial analysts fully understood that these environmental, political, and social aspects could not really be made calculable in a way it could be done with some of the financial data they were operating with. Still, they put a lot of effort into putting these aspects into a format that could at least be illustrated in charts or tables in a company report. The reason behind this is that, once these data could be depicted as market signals, they allowed a certain degree of comparability and interchangeability.

Such processes of economization can be understood as part of a broader process that Karl Polanyi ([1944] 1957) called the great transformation. To Polanyi, the great transformation was the movement away from a world in which economic life is embedded in social life and toward a world where social life is embedded in economic life. Polanyi says this transformation is a political project that aims to create a market society, that is, a society underpinned by the economic imperative (see Hann and Hart 2009; Hart and Ortiz 2008). This is where the broader influence of financial analysts in public discourse becomes apparent. Their approaches reframe the way we look at social, environmental, political, or cultural processes. In so doing, they help to integrate an economistic ideology into public discourse.

· 9 ·

Why the Economy
Needs Narratives

I started this book with a simple paradox: If there is the common assumption among economists that financial markets are efficient and market developments thus cannot be predicted, why do financial analysts exist? Studying financial analysts and their market practice on an everyday level, I aimed to draw an ethnographic picture of the people whose activities put in question one of the cornerstones of Chicago-style neoclassical economics and the conviction of many market fundamentalists.

In the empirical part of the book, I approached the work of financial analysts by illustrating their working environment, their valuation practices, and their role as market intermediaries. We saw how financial analysts become a professional subgroup by differentiating themselves from other financial market participants. Using cultural codes, such as ways of speaking, dressing, and presenting themselves, they embrace the role of experts in a market setting and distance themselves from other bankers. In so doing, they create symbolic power that allows them to become influential in the market setting. They highlight their expertise by stressing their superior education and their ability to analyze financial markets through the use of complex calculative approaches and in-depth knowledge.

Referring to their market practice, I described how financial analysts construct investment narratives that can be made explicit and sold to investors. Rather than being based on calculation and collection of information alone, these investment narratives arise from an eclectic mix of affective elements, implicit strategies, and experimenting around with various calculative approaches. Only when made explicit, for example when consulting investors or in investment reports, these investment narratives are rephrased to become coherent. Good analysts are defined by their ability to construct and communicate such investment narratives. Their success does not primarily lie in narratives turning out to be true, but in whether these narratives reinforce the financial analyst's ability to understand markets and convince others of his or her particular perspective on the future of markets.

Turning to the other stakeholders of Swiss Bank, we saw how investment narratives circulate within Swiss Bank and how they find their way into public discourse. Their intermediary role makes financial analysts useful to wealth managers and the host bank. Wealth managers can use investment narratives to communicate to clients and create the impression that their investment strategies are based on expert knowledge. For Swiss Bank as the host institution, in turn, financial analysts are animators who persuade clients to continuously buy and sell stocks by creating ever-changing investment recommendations. In public discourse, financial analysts also play another important role: Through the performance of their expertise, they give the impression that there are ways of navigating financial markets that are not speculative but based on reason.

Market Practice and Performative Effects

Before I focused on the empirical level of forecasting, I started my book by giving an introduction to the performativity concept, which has become a popular theory to think about financial markets from a social science perspective. I argued that unlike the studies conducted by scholars adhering to this theory, financial analysis cannot be understood as a market practice that emerges from the theoretical assumptions of economists. The reason is that, if the efficient market hypothesis would be performative in a way it is described in the social studies of finance, financial analysts would not exist.

Drawing from the empirical findings presented in this book, I would like to complicate this thought and state that the example of financial analysis does not necessarily have to be understood as contradicting performativity theory, but as a starting point to enhance it.

The first reason to call for such an enhancement is the fact that analysts sometimes become *enactors* of market efficiency. When thinking about the efficient market hypothesis, one thing is of particular interest: When economists such as Samuelson or Fama claim that all publicly available information is always already reflected in the price, they conceal the fact that this reflection of information must be done by someone or something. There are two jokes that critical economists like to tell with regard to this point. The first joke is about a neoclassical economist walking down the street with a friend. When the friend sees a hundred-dollar bill lying on the ground and wants to pick it up, the economist says, "Don't bother—if it was a genuine hundred dollar bill, someone would have already picked it up." The other joke goes like this: "How many neoclassical economists does it take to change a light bulb? None. They sit in the dark and wait for the market to do it."

The absence of a discussion on the human activities or devices that lead to the process of pricing in information is indeed striking. Proponents of the neoclassical economic school of thought often argue that the market, understood as some kind of *macroanthropos*, autonomously integrates publicly available information into market prices. If we assume, however, that the market is simply the entirety of aggregated activities of individual market actors, we can claim that, among the various actors and their activities, financial analysis is the market practice that integrates new information into the market by gathering and analyzing it. Neoclassical economists do not make this enactment of market efficiency explicit. Still, it is the foundation of why markets can be understood as being efficient in the first place (see Ortiz 2013).

A second reason not to simply ignore the performativity theory when thinking about financial analysis is the fact that *there are* performative effects to be observed when studying the work of financial analysts. Various examples put forward in this book showed how the knowledge that emerges from financial analysis as a market practice can shape markets—the object it aims to describe. The more investors accept a particular investment narrative to be legitimate, the more the outcome of the entirety of investment activities will be influenced by this investment narrative. Markets may thus develop in the direction that analysts think they will develop, which can make investment narratives self-fulfilling prophecies.

This performative effect, however, does not take place between economic theory and economic practice, but between the knowledge produced by financial analysis as a market practice and the market as an empirical fact. This form of performativity corresponds to the one Douglas Holmes (2014) has described when studying the role of central bankers. In his example, the formatting of markets also does not take place between economic theory and markets as an empirical fact, but between the utterances of central bankers and the markets. If central bankers claim that markets will recover, for example, they increase the chance that market in fact will recover, because market participants adjust their ways of acting in the market to the scenario advanced by central bankers.

The reflexivity of markets is located between market practitioners who act as experts, such as central bankers or financial analysts, and other market participants who follow their expert advice. To integrate these processes into existing theory, the performativity concept should thus differentiate between the realm of academic knowledge, practical knowledge, and markets as an empirical fact. Although in some cases markets may be formatted by academic knowledge (as it is illustrated by many scholars from the social studies of finance), markets also can be formatted by practical knowledge that emerges from market practices. The cases of central bankers and financial analysts both correspond to the latter form of performativity.[1]

Narration and Market Agency

The data presented in this book can thus add to the enhancement of the performativity concept, but my main line of argumentation focused on something different: the role of narratives in financial analysis. Throughout the empirical part of the book, I have shown that financial analysis is a market practice that aims to create investment narratives and that these investment narratives, in turn, lead to analysts being perceived as legitimate market actors. As I aimed to illustrate, all the activities of financial analysts ultimately lead to the performance of their role as narrators.

As narrators, financial analysts help construct a sense of meaning in market movements. To achieve the status of narrators, they first have to establish themselves as financial experts rather than as "bankers."

Once accepted as experts, financial analysts can cultivate an image of being able to understand markets and can therefore encourage other market participants to *invest* rather than *speculate*. Even if, from an analytical perspective, investment and speculation are both forms of capitalist action that engage with uncertain futures (see Bear 2015), financial analysts cultivate a differentiation between investment and speculation that goes back to Graham and Dodd's(1940, 106) claim that investment, unlike speculation, is based on "thorough analysis." By engaging in this thorough analysis, financial analysts create the idea that their work can turn speculators into investors and that their calculative, cultural, and social practices signify that they can detect a sense of meaning in market movements.

The investment narratives that analysts construct thus allow other market participants to think of market movements as developing predictably, rather than randomly. To achieve this, analysts must became experts in the art of narration. Once investment narratives are constructed, they create a benefit for other actors who belong to the same organization. As I illustrated it, this is the case for wealth managers and the host bank, who use the analysts' narratives to make clients invest, to externalize failure, or to generate fees.

Also, the work of analysts creates a sense of agency in an environment of radical uncertainty. In this kind of environment, being active rather than passive appears to be psychologically important. The narratives of financial analysts suggest that investors, by either adapting or rejecting them, can become active decision makers and can influence the profitability of their investments. Even though empirical research challenges the economic utility of active investing (see French 2008; Marti and Scherer 2016), many investors seem to prefer to be active market participants. Financial analysts provide them with the tools to do so.

Here it is important to note that the role of financial analysts as creators of a sense of agency is not limited to the investors alone. The host bank, the wealth managers, the analysts themselves, and any other participants in the market like to think that they have the power and the tools to actively navigate through a market environment that is unstable and uncertain. It can therefore be said that financial analysts produce a setting in which all market participants can become active decision makers.

Why the Financial Market Economy Needs Narratives

The central role that narratives play in financial analysis reveals something important about the way the economy works that goes beyond the work of financial analysts: The economy needs narratives, because they make the unknowable future accessible to investors in the present.

As Beckert (2013, 2016) points out, imagining the unknowable future plays a critical role in all current economic activities that take place in current capitalism. By assessing the present and anticipating the future, financial market participants create financial opportunities. Assume, for example, that you have one hundred US dollars that you can invest in the stock market. Would to buy Apple shares, because the iPhone is fashionable? Or Roche shares, because they are the leaders in the development of cancer medication? If you are new to financial markets, someone will eventually tell you that the very fact that a company is successful does not grant you satisfactory revenue. The reason is that many investors before you also chose Apple and Roche shares for the very same reason and increased the share price by buying those stocks. Apple's fashionability and Roche's success in cancer medication is thus already priced in. To you as an investor, this means that, in order to generate revenue, you should not simply consider companies that are successful today, but companies that might be successful *in the future*. Will the iPhone continue to be fashionable? Will Roche stay a leading company in the development of cancer medication? Or will new companies, whose success is not priced in yet, become the next Apple or Roche?

You see where this is going: In order to be a successful investor, you have to create an expectation about the unknowable future. The same is true for many of the other activities that characterize the economy. As Beckert (2013) states, credit relations, for example, are based on the expectation of whether the person a credit is given to will be able to pay it back at some stage in the future. Innovation is based on the same logic. To be innovative, an entrepreneur has to create an expectation about a future demand he or she wants to meet. This future demand cannot be accessed through calculation, but through narratives that indicate how a future demand might look.

Understanding economic action in a financial market setting as directed toward the future is not a new claim. In 1921, Frank Knight famously stated that risk and uncertainty represent two categories that are central to economic activity organized around financial markets. As Knight argued, risk represents a measurable category and can be quantified by probability calculation, but uncertainty cannot be expressed in numbers at all. Both categories are directed toward the future, aiming to anticipate economic developments in order to generate profit. Knight's actual argument of his book *Risk, Uncertainty, and Profit* (1921)—and this has not been as much discussed as the distinction between risk and uncertainty—is that in a financial market economy, economic actors must always engage in *both* risk *and* uncertainty. This, Knight claims, differentiates economic action in a financial market setting from economic action in nonmarket settings, that is, for example, economic exchange of a good against cash between two persons.[2]

To engage in the unknowable future is thus the foundation of economic action in a financial market economy. This becomes apparent also when looking at financial market instruments such as derivatives. As Appadurai (2016, 2) illustrates, derivatives are essentially "promise[s] about the uncertain future" (see also Esposito 2011; LiPuma and Lee 2004; Maurer 2002). Their value lies in the future development of an underlying asset. As my example of Apple and Roche illustrates, the same is true for stock market investment. The value of investment lies in the future development of a stock, rather than in the present profitability of a company.

The future, whether it be economic or not, can be made accessible in the present only through narratives on how something might turn out to be. In financial markets, in which the only way to make profit is by anticipating the future, participants thus depend on narratives that make the future accessible. The practice of creating market forecasts is a critical technique that enables investors to engage in speculative endeavors. In this sense, neoclassical economists are, quite simply, wrong about their efforts to challenge the role of financial analysts. Although their market practice may not always help to predict how the *actual future* turns out to be, their narratives are the very central tools that make *possible futures* accessible to market participants in the present. Financial analysis is thus not a negligible market practice. Quite the contrary: Their investment narratives are the starting point in any financial market activity and, as pointed to by Comaroff and Comaroff (2000), a defining feature of neoliberal culture.

Methodological Appendix

For the fieldwork that serves as the basis to this book, I became a member of Swiss Bank's research program. The program allows academics to collect empirical data inside the corporation and at the same time actively participate in the bank's working processes. During the two years of the research program (from September 2010 to August 2012), I became an integral part of the analysts' community. I learned the language, the cultural codes, the working procedures, and the daily routines of financial analysts.

For an anthropologist without any track record in banking, it would probably have been impossible to enter this world of wealth for fieldwork purposes. Luckily, I financed my studies in anthropology by working as a temporary staff member at a French and then a US bank in Zurich. As a result, I knew how I had to dress, speak, and act to be accepted as a peer by other bankers. This helped me approach the field's "gatekeepers" (Abolafia 1998, 78) in a way that made them see me as someone who was already familiar with the field. Moreover, I wrote my master's thesis on Islamic finance (for results, see Leins 2010), a topic in which Swiss Bank was particularly interested. As a result of my banking experience and my knowledge of Islamic finance, Swiss Bank's human resources department accepted my application for Swiss Bank's research program.

Being active in the financial analysis department allowed me to do participant observation without constantly being perceived as an outsider. Because I was able to move freely around the department and, to some extent, the bank as a whole, I had access to a tremendous amount of intriguing ethnographic data. I kept a research diary for the two years I was with the bank and noted all observations, impressions, and data gathered. The data I use in this book stem from observations and participation in meetings, training sessions, informal discussions, business lunches, and after-work drinks. Furthermore, I analyzed written documents, banking guidelines, manuals on working processes, and the internal structures of Swiss Bank. Last but not least, the results presented in this book also were generated by the knowledge I acquired when acting as a financial analyst myself during my fieldwork. Cognitive anthropologist Maurice Bloch (1998, 22–26) uses the term *introspection* to describe this practice of generating data by temporarily internalizing a particular lifestyle.

Unlike many other anthropologists, I did not do any formal interviews during my fieldwork. I made this decision because I had worked with interviews before and was not satisfied with the depth of data I received from interviewing people in banking. The main reason was that many financial market participants are well-educated and well-trained speakers. When being interviewed by an anthropologist, they are well aware of what the anthropologist expects them to say, and it happens that they formulate things in a way that they believe reflects what the anthropologist wants to hear. This game of social expectations makes conversation easy but limits the validity of data. In interviews for a former study I conducted, it was always hard to avoid being treated as a journalist looking for catchy quotes for a newspaper article. The situation was similar when I studied financial analysts. They frequently talk to journalists and receive expert training on how to talk to the mass media and people from outside the banking sector. Because I had the opportunity to stay with the bank for two years, I decided to fully concentrate on participant observation, informal talks, and document analysis.

Doing ethnographic research is often a complicated endeavor. In my case, becoming a member of Swiss Bank's research program to conduct my fieldwork created a number of methodological and ethical challenges. With regard to the methodology, for example, I encountered difficulties in defining the scope of my field. Swiss Bank has a large number of employees located in all the large financial centers of the world. Being geographically close to a person does not necessarily mean working in a similar area of banking. In the case of the financial analysis department, some of the employees were located in

London, Dubai, and Singapore (see chapter 4 for a description of the geographical setup of the financial analysis department).

Another difficulty was that I continually had to try to dissociate myself from the dominant economic explanatory narratives that analysts enjoy telling. Because I aimed to look at financial analysis as a market practice from an anthropological perspective, I had to learn to "diseconomize," as Latour (2013, 385) would say, in order to understand the economy. Reducing complex issues to easy and straightforward economic explanations is part of an analyst's job. There was almost no question I could ask that they could not answer in just a few sentences. This regularly challenged my efforts to critically reflect on their narratives and avoid imitating their particular ways of explaining things.

In terms of research ethics, I want to point to the fact that I had a research agreement with Swiss Bank that permitted me to collect ethnographic data in the bank and guaranteed my academic freedom. Of course, however, collecting data in a field where inside information can be very powerful and easily misused for political or economic interests meant that I had to proceed with a great deal of caution so as not to imperil my host institution, my interlocutors, or myself. As a result, I have anonymized all names (including the host institution's name) in the book and taken possible conflicts of interest into account during the writing phase.

Notes

Chapter One

1. Many of the informal conversations mentioned in this book were originally held in Swiss German. I have translated and paraphrased them.

2. Throughout the book, I use the term "financial market economy" to denominate the current economy, which is organized around financial markets as the settings in which value is negotiated and exchange takes place (see Epstein 2005). In *Banking on Words*, Appadurai (2016) uses the terms "financial capitalism" or "financialized capitalism" to point to the same frame of reference.

3. With regard to the efficient market hypothesis, I am not saying that I assume that markets are actually always efficient in reallocating resources. Scholars such as Stiglitz (Gale and Stiglitz 1989; Grossman and Stiglitz 1980) have convincingly argued that markets are, in fact, almost never fully efficient. In the case of financial analysis, there are also *informational asymmetries* that can be used to speculate on future market developments. Thus, my elaborations on market efficiency are not based on the fact that I support the theory, but on my interest in how financial analysis as a practical field can exist despite the fact that their practice is fiercely challenged by neoclassical economics.

4. I choose to talk about narratives rather than stories to highlight that, first, they do not necessarily have to be verbalized, second, they should be understood as culturally and socially constructed, and, third, they are always influenced by the positioning of the speaker who constructs and communicates them. For a detailed discussion of the conceptualization of narratives, see Carroll and Gibson (2011), Maggio (2014), Tanner (2016), and Zigon (2012).

5. I use the term "analyst" to designate a job description, not a grade. Some US-based banks use the term "analysts" as a grade for young professionals. Often, these analysts do bookkeeping rather than financial analysis.

6. In some ways, the concept of performativity seems to refer to the same effect that Robert K. Merton (1948) has called a self-fulfilling prophecy. Indeed, some scholars who write about how theory affects the practical world choose to describe the effects as self-fulfilling, rather than as performative. In management studies,

for example, Ferraro, Pfeffer, and Sutton (2005) argue that economic theory can become self-fulfilling if it is able to influence social norms in a market setting. Callon and MacKenzie, however, differentiate between self-fulfilling and performative effects, arguing that self-fulfilling prophecies are limited to the (conscious) beliefs of individual actors. Performativity, on the other hand, describes the incorporation of economic theory into the actors' beliefs and into the infrastructure of a market as a whole (Callon 2007, 321–24; MacKenzie 2006, 19).

7. I choose to use the term *affect*, rather than the analysts' native term *feeling*, or other similar terms, such as *sentiment* or *emotion*. As Shouse (2005; italics in the original) explains, "Feelings are *personal* and *biographical*, emotions are *social*, and affects are *prepersonal*." Affect is thus more abstract than feeling or emotion. Shouse defines affect as "a non-conscious experience of intensity; [. . .] a moment of unformed and unstructured potential." Analytically speaking, it is thus affect, rather than feeling or emotion, that influences the work of financial analysts when constructing narratives. Tacit knowledge, which is a second term I introduce here, is a term originally coined by Michael Polanyi ([1966] 2009) to denominate a type of knowledge that is hard to verbalize.

8. In his presidential address at the annual meeting of the American Economic Association on January 7, 2017, Robert Shiller introduced "narrative economics" as a concept that points to some of the issues I am describing in my book. Shiller (2017, 3) defines narrative economics as "the study of the spread and dynamics of popular narratives, the stories, particularly those of human interest and emotion, and how these change through time, to understand economic fluctuation." Shiller gives an intriguing account of how narratives can frame the perception of the economy and its development over time. In so doing, however, he does not examine the role of financial experts as producers of such narratives, but focuses on how narratives are spread once they have already been constructed.

Chapter Two

1. The concept of markets being solely governed by supply and demand is described in Adam Smith's famous notion of the invisible hand that matches supply and demand without any need for intervention (see Smith [1776] 1991, 351–52; Smith [1759] 2002, 215). As Graeber (2011, 50–51) points out, Smith originally thought of the invisible hand as the agent of divine providence, i.e., the hand of God.

2. See, among many, all the contributions in Mirowski and Plehwe 2009. For a critical discussion of the use of the term *neoliberalism* in anthropology, see Hilgers 2012, Wacquant 2012, and the subsequent debate in *Social Anthropology*.

3. For a detailed sociological account of the development and academic implications of these new theoretical concepts, see MacKenzie 2006, chapter 2.

4. Hayek also played a significant role as an ideological father of the theory. In "The Use of Knowledge in Society," Hayek (1945) states that the central function

of a market is to decentralize information. This, he says, leads to a situation where partial knowledge is used to benefit from market anomalies and ultimately results in the market price, having bundled all this partial knowledge, and becoming the ultimate authority.

5. Ironically, in the early 1990s, Fama and French (1992, 1993) introduced a "three-factor model" that states that companies with high risk, small capitalization and a low price-to-book ratio tend to outperform the overall market. In many ways, the three-factor model seems to contradict the assumption of the efficient market hypothesis. Fama, however, continuously stressed that the existence of short-term market "anomalies" supports his claim that markets are generally efficient.

6. One example is Mankiw's *Principles of Economics* (2015), which is among the most widely read introductory books of economics at the moment.

7. Unlike the other concepts coming from new institutional economic theory, the concept of transaction costs is now also used by a number of economists who consider themselves to be neoclassical economists.

Chapter Three

1. The history of Swiss banking could easily be the subject of a whole book and has been studied by economic historians such as Cassis (1992; Cassis and Tanner 1993), Guex (2000; Guex and Mazbouri 2010), Ritzmann (1973); and Tanner (1993, 1997). My introduction is thus just a short, and certainly incomplete, overview of some of the stages in Swiss banking's history.

2. As Cassis and Tanner (1992) point out, it would be misleading to look at the history of Swiss banking as a continuum stretching from Geneva's trade fair to today's banking. In fact, until the end of World War II at least, banking in Switzerland experienced radical disruptions.

3. As Harrington (2016) convincingly shows, this practice of secrecy still represents a central element of the work ethos of many wealth managers today.

4. The same is true for countries such as Sweden or Denmark. Switzerland, however, had a longer tradition of wealth management than these other countries that were also not directly involved in the two world wars.

5. This finding has caused a great deal of controversy in Switzerland, in that it contradicted a popular narrative that said Swiss bank secrecy was established to protect Jewish wealth stored in Switzerland from appropriation by the Nazis (Guex 2000, 239).

6. Many of the world's most ruthless dictators have hidden money in Swiss bank accounts. Some of the largest scandals involve the wealth of Haiti's Jean-Claude Duvalier, the Philippines' Imelda and Ferdinand Marcos, Zaire's Mobutu Sese Seko, Nigeria's Sani Abacha, Liberia's Charles Taylor, and Egypt's Hosni Mubarak.

7. During Swiss banking's structural shift in the 1990s and early 2000s, Swiss banks massively expanded their business activities in the United States. In 2006,

UBS employed more people in the United States than in Switzerland (Wetzel, Flück, and Hofstätter 2010, 351).

8. Here, the term toxic refers to the fact that the products no longer have a defined market price and therefore cannot be traded. It does not mean that they are worthless per se, but it reflects the absence of potential buyers for a certain time period.

9. The Swiss financial regulatory agency FINMA published a report on September 14, 2009, stating that, in view of the positive development of the economy in the years before the crisis, banks, politicians, and regulators misevaluated the state of the economy as a whole. As FINMA goes on, however, these financial actors were not guilty of misconduct by allowing Swiss banks to participate in increasingly aggressive and highly leveraged activities before the crisis.

10. I use the term "social role" (German: *Sozialfiguren*) to highlight the performative character of the ascriptions referring to identity. Unlike "identity," "stereotype," "image," and "self-ascription," the concept of social roles stresses the framing from outside as well as the embodiment and performance of the roles by the actors themselves (Moebius and Schroer 2010).

11. When creating the fictional character of Gordon Gekko, Oliver Stone was inspired by a number of real-life Wall Street figures (Ivan Boeski, Carl Icahn, and James Tomilson Hill are frequently mentioned). Gordon Gekko was by no means, however, a representation of an established social role in the 1980s. Ironically, as Oliver Stone recently remarked in an interview, the presentation of Gordon Gekko as an ultimately ruthless banker did not result in most Wall Street bankers distancing themselves from the character. In fact, the character served as a role model for young bankers who joined Wall Street in the 1980s ("Greed Never Left," 2010).

12. The Swiss military is not a professional organization but is organized as a militia.

13. These are native categories, that is, categories that are used by the private bankers themselves. I chose to use them as analytical categories as well.

14. See Boyer (2005) and Mason and Stoilkova (2012) for a discussion of the corporeality of expertise.

Chapter Four

1. The information used in this chapter is based on the bank's structure and employment rolls as they stood at the end of October 2011, which was more or less halfway through my fieldwork. During my two years of fieldwork, many new members joined the financial analysis team and others changed departments, were fired, or changed teams during restructuring processes. Rapid transformations and employee turnover, as well as ongoing restructuring processes, are a characteristic feature of flexible capitalism. Because of the ongoing transformation of my field site, the exact numbers and information are to be understood as a snapshot, rather than as a stable description of the financial analysis department at Swiss Bank.

2. Here it could be argued that these threadbare conditions represent an outcome of what Weber ([1905] 2009) calls "inner-worldly asceticism," which, to Weber, is part of the Protestant ethic that helped imposing modern capitalist thought.

3. Junk bonds, which are bonds with bad creditworthiness that are used for highly speculative purposes, are an exception.

4. It should be noted that summer internships are publicly tendered jobs in Switzerland. Unlike in the United States and the United Kingdom, they are not usually given away to the children or affiliates of the institution's clients.

Chapter Five

1. A number of scholars have stressed the role of valuation as a cultural practice (see, for example, Bessy and Chauvin 2013; Fourcade 2011; Helgesson and Muniesa 2013; Stark 2009). As Stark (2009, 7–8) notes, studying valuation means overcoming the former division of labor under which economists studied *value* and sociologists studied *values*. Recently, economic value has also become a central object of study in anthropology (see, for example, Graeber 2001, 2005; Gregory 2014).

2. Of course, some economists also point to the fact that market efficiency is achieved by human action. In this case, they usually stress the role of *arbitrage*, i.e., taking advantage of short-term price discrepancies to benefit from information asymmetries (see Miyazaki 2007).

3. Hertz (2000) calls this a logic of the third degree, because "Keynes' discomfort is with choices based not on what is 'really' the case, nor even on representations of what others 'genuinely' think is the case, but on representations of other people's representations, in which the reference to reality drops out entirely" (42). As Hertz argues, however, Keynes's discomfort with the separation of the real and the speculative in the economy should be understood as a complex ontology, rather than as given. Financial markets, Hertz states, certainly do deal with representations (and representations of representations). Their effects, however (social as well as material), are always to be seen as real (see Lépinay and Hertz 2005; Muniesa 2014, 22).

4. A similar construction and spread of consensus is described by Carlo Caduff (2015) as contagion.

5. Luhmann 1998; Rabinow 2008, 57–60; see also Caduff 2015; Leins 2013.

Chapter Six

1. In the original conversation held in Swiss German, Marco used the terms *gschpüre* and *gschpürsch mi*, which describe developing a feeling as well as the ability to sympathize with other people. This prosocial element led Marco to say that anthropologists are, by definition, good at developing feelings in a market context as well as in social interactions.

2. This phrase was coined by Warren Buffett, who was a scholar of Benjamin Graham.

3. These findings by no means support the currently popular view of financial markets as one big casino (generally expressed by the use of the term "casino capitalism"). As Cassidy (2009) illustrates, the difference between casino gambling and investing in stocks is that casino gambling involves only risk, not uncertainty. Referring to F. Knight (1921), who differentiated between risk (which is calculable) and uncertainty (which is not calculable), Cassidy argues that in casinos, gamblers deal only with calculable risk, although in financial markets, participants deal with risk as well as uncertainty (see Appadurai 2016). Also, the notion of the financial market as a casino is often used to denounce finance as a system that destroys value in contrast to the so-called real economy that creates value (see de Goede 2005 for a historical perspective on gambling and finance). Hertz and I (2012) have argued elsewhere that this is merely a romantic picture and that a differentiation between a speculative economy and a real economy fails to grasp the underlying logic of capitalism that embraces not only finance, but also the so-called real economy (see also Hertz 2000).

4. Of course, so-called free markets are never fully deregulated and democratic markets in which everybody can participate under the same conditions. It is worth recalling the critique put forward by new institutional economics that states that markets are always embedded in institutionalized power structures. This leads to the fact that some actors are empowered by the so-called free markets, while for others such free markets restrict their opportunities to operate freely. To stress this, I talk of free market narratives, rather than of free markets.

5. Financial analysts at Swiss Bank of course also offer analyses and forecasts for non-Swiss stocks. Here, the reporting times depend on the home country of the company that reports.

6. The exact design, as well as the name of the company and its CEO, have been anonymized in this sample report. The narrative itself and the market information shown in the reproduced report, however, are more or less identical to a company report published by Swiss Bank sometime in 2013. Quotations from the report retain the original spelling and grammar.

7. Here, it is interesting to note that the establishment of the analysts' investment strategies is both a collective and an individualistic approach. On the one hand, analysts have a shared repertoire of strategies and mnemonics to which they refer. Also, their view on how a free market is supposed to work is a collectively shared cognitive frame. In order to stress their agency, however, their approach has to be recognized as unique and individualistic. Therefore, they usually claim that they partly base their investment narrative on insights and beliefs that are not shared by other analysts. The use of original information in formulating a narrative, as I presented it in chapter 5, becomes important. By using information sources that are considered unique and original, financial analysts stress their role as individually skilled experts who adopt an approach that cannot be easily copied by other financial analysts.

Chapter Seven

1. I have changed the original name of the concept in order to protect anonymity.

2. Microfinance, in which very small amounts of money are lent to people who cannot otherwise access financial markets, emerged in the late 1970s as a concept invented by Muhammad Yunus. In 2006, Yunus and Grameen Bank were jointly awarded the Nobel Peace Prize for their activity in reducing poverty through microloans. The tremendously high interest charged by microfinance institutions, however, and the practice of collective custody, has led economists as well as anthropologists to criticize microfinance. Some argue that microfinance can empower poor people to set up businesses, but others see it as a neoliberal strategy to expand debt and financial dependency globally (see Elyachar 2005, 2012; Rankin and Shakya 2007).

3. This quote cannot officially be traced back to Milton Friedman, but it is often used and ascribed to him in financial market publications and academic papers. See, for example, Smith and Thurman 2007, 34.

4. In experimental economics, the research of Falk and Szech (2013) supports the assumption that market processes can lead to an externalization of responsibilities and can marginalize the role of moral values. In a paper published in the renowned journal *Science*, the two economists present the results of an experiment in which they compared the willingness of actors to consider moral values in a market and a nonmarket situation. Each of the participants was given a mouse, which they could kill for a financial payoff. Presenting multiple variations of the experiments, the authors show that, in nonmarket situations, it takes a relatively high payoff to make people kill their mice. The payoff significantly decreases, however, if the participants can trade payoffs and mice in a market situation. The authors conclude that "market interaction displays a tendency to lower moral values, relative to individually stated preferences" (710).

Chapter Eight

1. The Swiss Bankers Association (*Schweizer Bankiervereinigung / Association Suisse des Banquiers*) is the umbrella organization of all Swiss financial institutions. Although mainly a lobbying organization, the association sometimes develops directives that are later referred to by the Swiss financial regulatory agency FINMA.

2. "Chinese wall" is a term that is frequently used in banks to describe the spatial and informational separation of banking units required by regulatory guidelines.

3. This aim to regulate access to knowledge is interesting because it shows that the persons who have authored and enforced these codes have been well aware of the reflexive nature of capitalism, i.e., the fact that actors' access to information impacts financial realities (see Thrift 2005). Also, these regulations show how,

through standardizing information access, an informationally efficient market is enacted (see Ortiz 2013).

4. Of course, the optimistic bias of the analysts is also reinforced by the fact that stock market analysts at Swiss Bank cannot recommend structured products or put options. By recommending put options, which are financial instruments that take advantage of falling stock prices, analysts would be able to show clients how to financially benefit from a decreasing market. Without the option of recommending structured products and put options, a buy recommendation is the only way to make investors benefit financially in the short term.

5. As Daromir Rudnyckyj mentioned in a personal conversation, my book shows that in fact B sometimes leads back to A and transforms A. When talking about the logic of economics, Anne is thus oblivious to the reflexivity of her own practices.

6. For the role of experts in defining and capitalizing on the notion of crisis, see Caduff 2014 and 2015.

7. Commodification is a concept that is usually accredited to Karl Marx, even though Marx never used the term himself. In the first volume of *Capital: A Critique of Political Economy* ([1867] 1990), however, he gives a precise introduction on how, in capitalism, goods take on a commodity form in order to become tradable in markets.

Chapter Nine

1. Callon (2007) has pointed to this fact when he differentiated between "confined economists" and "economist in the wild." To my knowledge, this differentiation has not, however, been picked up in most of the empirical studies on performativity.

2. Joseph Schumpeter ([1911] 2012) makes a similar point when claiming that innovation cannot be based on calculative approaches, because innovation cannot be deduced from existing knowledge but only from imaginaries of the future (Beckert 2013, 328–29; see also Bear 2015).

References

Abolafia, Mitchel Y. 1996. *Making Markets: Opportunism and Restraint on Wall Street*. Cambridge, MA: Harvard University Press.

———. 1998. "Markets as Cultures: An Ethnographic Approach." In *The Laws of the Markets*, edited by Michel Callon, 69–85. Oxford, UK: Blackwell.

Acheson, James M. 1994. "Welcome to Nobel Country: A Review of Institutional Economics." In *Anthropology and Institutional Economics: Monographs in Economic Anthropology*, edited by James M. Acheson, 3–42. Lanham, MD: University Press of America.

Akerlof, George, and Robert J. Shiller. 2009. *Animal Spirits: How Human Psychology Drives the Economy, and Why It Matters for Global Capitalism*. Princeton, NJ: Princeton University Press.

Appadurai, Arjun. 2016. *Banking on Words: The Failure of Language in the Age of Derivative Finance*. Chicago: University of Chicago Press.

Bardhan, Ashok, and Dwight Jaffee. 2011. "Globalization of R&D: Offshoring Innovative Activity to Emerging Economies." In *Global Outsourcing and Offshoring: An Integrated Approach to Theory and Corporate Strategy*, edited by Farok J. Contractor, Vikas Kumar, Sumit K. Kundu, and Torben Pedersen, 48–72. Cambridge: Cambridge University Press.

Barry, Andrew, and Don Slater. 2002. "Technology, Politics and the Market: An Interview with Michel Callon." *Economy and Society* 31 (2): 285–306.

Baumann, Claude. 2006. *Ausgewaschen: Die Schweizer Banken am Wendepunkt*. Zurich: Xanthippe.

Bear, Laura. 2014a. "Capital and Time: Uncertainty and Qualitative Measures of Inequality." *British Journal of Sociology* 65 (4): 639–49.

———. 2014b. "Doubt, Conflict, Mediation: The Anthropology of Modern Time." *Journal of the Royal Anthropological Institute* 20 (1): 3–30.

———. 2015. "Capitalist Divination: Populist-Speculators and Technologies of Imagination on the Hooghly River." *Comparative Studies in South Asia, Africa and the Middle East* 35 (3): 408–23.

———. 2016. "Time as Technique." *Annual Review of Anthropology* 45:487–502.

Beckert, Jens. 2013. "Capitalism as a System of Expectations: Toward a Sociological Microfoundation of Political Economy." *Politics and Society* 41 (3): 323–50.

———. 2016. *Imagined Futures: Fictional Expectations and Capitalist Dynamics.* Cambridge, MA: Harvard University Press.

Beckert, Jens, and Hartmut Berghoff. 2013. "Risk and Uncertainty in Financial Markets: A Symposium." *Socio-Economic Review* 11 (3): 497–99.

Bergier, Jean-François. 1990. *Wirtschaftsgeschichte der Schweiz: Von den Anfängen bis zur Gegenwart.* 2nd ed. Zurich: Benziger.

Bessy, Christian, and Pierre-Marie Chauvin. 2013. "The Power of Market Intermediaries: From Information to Valuation Processes." *Valuation Studies* 1 (1): 83–117.

Beunza, Daniel, and Raghu Garud. 2007. "Calculators, Lemmings or Frame-Makers? The Intermediary Role of Securities Analysts." In *Market Devices*, edited by Michel Callon, Yuval Millo, and Fabian Muniesa, 13–39. Malden, MA: Blackwell.

Beunza, Daniel, and David Stark. 2004. "Tools of the Trade: The Socio-Technology of Arbitrage in a Wall Street Trading Room." *Industrial and Corporate Change* 13 (2): 369–400.

Bloch, Maurice E. F. 1998. *How We Think They Think: Anthropological Approaches to Cognition, Memory and Literacy.* Boulder, CO: Westview.

Bodie, Zvi, Alex Kane, and Alan J. Marcus. 2002. *Investments.* 5th ed. New York: McGraw-Hill.

Bogle, John C. 2008. "A Question So Important that It Should Be Hard to Think about Anything Else." *Journal of Portfolio Management* 34 (2): 95–102.

Bonhage, Barbara, Hanspeter Lussy, and Marc Perrenoud. 2001. *Nachrichtenlose Vermögen bei Schweizer Banken: Depots, Konten und Safes von Opfern des national-sozialistischen Regimes und Restitutionsprobleme in der Nachkriegszeit.* Veröffentlichungen der UEK, Band 15. Zurich: Chronos.

Bourdieu, Pierre. 1984. *Distinction: A Social Critique of the Judgement of Taste.* Cambridge, MA: Harvard University Press.

Boyer, Dominic. 2005. "The Corporeality of Expertise." *Ethnos* 70 (2): 243–66.

———. 2008. "Thinking Through the Anthropology of Experts." *Anthropology in Action* 15 (2): 38–46.

Brinton, Mary C., and Victor Nee, eds. 1998. *The New Institutionalism in Sociology.* Stanford, CA: Stanford University Press.

Bröckling, Ulrich. 2016. *The Entrepreneurial Self: Fabricating a New Type of Subject.* London: Sage.

Bruce, Brian. 2002. "Stock Analysts: Experts on Whose Behalf?" *Journal of Psychology and Financial Markets* 3 (4): 198–201.

Bundesgesetz über die Banken und Sparkassen. 1934. "Bundesgesetz über die Banken und Sparkassen (Bankengesetz, BankG)." November 8. http://www.admin.ch/opc/de/classified-compilation/19340083/index.html.

Butler, Judith. 2010. "Performative Agency." *Journal of Cultural Economy* 3 (2): 147–61.

Caduff, Carlo. 2014. "Pandemic Prophecy, or How to Have Faith in Reason." *Current Anthropology* 55 (3): 296–315.

———. 2015. *The Pandemic Perhaps: Dramatic Events in a Public Culture of Danger.* Oakland: University of California Press.

Çalışkan, Koray, and Michel Callon. 2009. "Economization, Part 1: Shifting Attention from the Economy towards Processes of Economization." *Economy and Society* 38 (3): 369–98.

———. 2010. "Economization, Part 2: A Research Programme for the Study of Markets." *Economy and Society* 39 (1): 1–32.

Callon, Michel. 1998. "Introduction: The Embeddedness of Economic Markets in Economics." In *The Laws of the Markets*, edited by Michel Callon, 1–57. Oxford, UK: Blackwell.

———. 2007. "What Does It Mean to Say That Economics Is Performative?" In *Do Economists Make Markets? On the Performativity of Economics*, edited by Donald MacKenzie, Fabian Muniesa, and Lucia Siu, 311–57. Princeton; NJ: Princeton University Press.

Carrier, James G. 1997. *Meanings of the Market: The Free Market in Western Culture.* New York: Berg.

———. 2012. Introduction to *Ethical Consumption: Social Value and Economic Practice*, edited by James G. Carrier and Peter G. Luetchford, 1–36. New York: Berghahn.

Carroll, Noël, and John Gibson, eds. 2011. *Narrative, Emotion, and Insight.* University Park, PA: Pennsylvania State University Press.

Carruthers, Bruce G., and Wendy Nelson Espeland. 1991. "Accounting for Rationality: Double-Entry Bookkeeping and the Rhetoric of Economic Rationality." *American Journal of Sociology* 97 (1): 31 69.

Cartwright, Edward. 2011. *Behavioral Economics.* London: Routledge.

Cassidy, Rebecca. 2009. "'Casino Capitalism' and the Financial Crisis." *Anthropology Today* 25 (4): 10–13.

Cassidy, Rebecca, Andrea Pisac, and Claire Loussouarn, eds. 2013. *Qualitative Research in Gambling: Exploring the Production and Consumption of Risk.* London: Routledge.

Cassis, Youssef, ed. 1992. *Finance and Financiers in European History 1880–1960.* Paris: Éditions de la Maison des Sciences de l'Homme; Cambridge: Cambridge University Press.

Cassis, Youssef, and Jakob Tanner. 1992. "Finance and Financiers in Switzerland, 1880–1960 (with Fabienne Debrunner)." In *Finance and Financiers in European History 1880–1960*, edited by Youssef Cassis, 293–316. Paris: Éditions de la Maison des Sciences de l'Homme; Cambridge: Cambridge University Press.

———, eds. 1993. *Banken und Kredit in der Schweiz (1850–1930).* Zurich: Chronos.

Chesney, Marc. 2014. *Vom Grossen Krieg zur Permanenten Krise: Der Aufstieg der Finanzaristokratie und das Versagen der Demokratie*. Zurich: Versus.

Chiapello, Eve. 2015. "Financialisation of Valuation." *Human Studies* 38 (1): 13–35.

Chong, Kimberly, and David Tuckett. 2015. "Constructing Conviction through Action and Narrative: How Money Managers Manage Uncertainty and the Consequence for Financial Market Functioning." *Socio-Economic Review* 13 (2): 309–30.

Coase, Ronald H. 1937. "The Nature of the Firm." *Economica* 4 (16): 386–405.

Comaroff, Jean, and John L. Comaroff. 2000. "Millennial Capitalism: First Thoughts on a Second Coming." *Public Culture* 12 (2): 291–343.

Commons, John R. 1924. *Legal Foundations of Capitalism*. New York: Macmillan.

Copeland, Tom, Tim Koller, and Jack Murrin. 2000. *Valuation: Measuring and Managing the Value of Companies*. 3rd ed. New York: Wiley.

Cowles, Alfred 3rd. 1933. "Can Stock Market Forecasters Forecast?" *Econometrica* 1 (3): 309–24.

"Currency Wars." 2010. *Economist*, October 16. http://www.economist.com /printedition/2010-10-16.

De Goede, Marieke. 2005. *Virtue, Fortune, Faith: A Genealogy of Finance*. Minneapolis, MN: University of Minnesota Press.

Dreman, David. 2002. "Analysts' Conflicts-of-Interest: Some Behavioral Aspects." *Journal of Psychology and Financial Markets* 3 (3): 138–40.

Elyachar, Julia. 2005. *Markets of Dispossession: NGOs, Economic Development, and the State in Cairo*. Durham, NC: Duke University Press.

———. 2012. "Before (and after) Neoliberalism: Tacit Knowledge, Secret of the Trade, and the Public Sector in Egypt." *Cultural Anthropology* 27 (1): 76–96.

Ensminger, Jean. 1992. *Making a Market: The Institutional Transformation of an African Society*. Cambridge: Cambridge University Press.

Epstein, Gerard. 2005. "Introduction: Financialization and the World Economy." In *Financialization and the World Economy*, edited by Gerard Epstein, 3–16. Cheltenham, UK: Edward Elgar.

Esposito, Elena. 2011. *The Future of Futures: The Time of Money in Financing and Society*. Cheltenham, UK: Edward Elgar.

Evans-Pritchard, Edward E. 1937. *Witchcraft, Oracles and Magic among the Azande*. Oxford, UK: Clarendon Press.

Falk, Armin, and Nora Szech. 2013. "Morals and Markets." *Science* 340:707–11.

Fama, Eugene F. 1965. "The Behavior of Stock-Market Prices." *Journal of Business* 38 (1): 34–105.

———. 1970. "Efficient Capital Markets: A Review of Theory and Empirical Work." *Journal of Finance* 25 (2): 383–417.

Fama, Eugene F., and Kenneth R. French. 1992. "The Cross-Section of Expected Stock Returns." *Journal of Finance* 47 (2): 427–65.

———. 1993. "Common Risk Factors in the Return on Stocks and Bonds." *Journal of Financial Economics* 33 (1): 3–56.

Ferraro, Fabrizio, Jeffrey Pfeffer, and Robert I. Sutton. 2005. "Economics, Language and Assumptions: How Theories Can Become Self-Fulfilling." *Academy of Management Review* 30 (1): 8–24.

Finke, Peter. 2005. *Nomaden im Transformationsprozess: Kasachen in der Post-Sozialistischen Mongolei.* Münster, Ger.: LIT.

———. 2014. *Variations on Uzbek Identity: Strategic Choices, Cognitive Schemas, and Political Constraint in Identification Processes.* New York: Berghahn.

FINMA. 2008. "Rundschreiben 2008/10: Selbstregulierung als Mindeststandard." November 20. https://www.finma.ch/de/~/media/finma/dokumente/dokumentencenter/myfinma/rundschreiben/finma-rs-2008-10.pdf?la=de.

Foucault, Michel. 2008. *The Birth of Biopolitics: Lectures at the Collège de France, 1978–1979.* Houndmills, UK: Palgrave Macmillan.

Fourcade, Marion. 2011. "Cents and Sensibility: Economic Valuation and the Nature of 'Nature.'" *American Journal of Sociology* 116 (6): 1721–77.

Francini, Esther Tisa, Anja Heuss, and Georg Kreis. 2001. *Fluchtgut—Raubgut: Der Transfer von Kulturgütern in und über die Schweiz 1933–1945 und die Frage der Restitution.* Veröffentlichungen der UEK, Band 1. Zurich: Chronos.

Free by 50. 2009. "Jim Cramer versus a Monkey: Who Wins?" April 21. http://www.freeby50.com/2009/04/jim-cramer-versus-monkey-who-wins.html.

French, Kenneth R. 2008. "Presidential Address: The Cost of Active Investing." *Journal of Finance* 63 (2): 1537–73.

Friedman, Milton. 1962. *Capitalism and Freedom.* Chicago: University of Chicago Press.

Friedman, Milton, and Rose D. Friedman. 1990. *Free to Choose: A Personal Statement.* Orlando, FL: Harcourt.

Furubotn, Eirik G., and Rudolf Richter. 2005. *Institutions and Economic Theory: The Contributions of the New International Economics.* 2nd ed. Ann Arbor: University of Michigan Press.

Gale, Ian, and Joseph E. Stiglitz. 1989. "A Simple Proof That Futures Markets Are Almost Always Informationally Inefficient." National Bureau of Economic Research, Working Paper No. 3209.

Garcia-Parpet, Marie-France. (1986) 2007. "The Social Construction of a Perfect Market: The Strawberry Auction at Fontaines-en-Sologne." In *Do Economists Make Markets? On the Performativity of Economics*, edited by Donald MacKenzie, Fabian Muniesa, and Lucia Siu, 20–53. Princeton; NJ: Princeton University Press.

Garsten, Christina. 2012. "Corporate Social Responsibility and Cultural Practices in Globalizing Markets." In *A Companion to the Anthropology of Europe*, edited by Ullrich Kockel, Máiread Nic Craith, and Jonas Frykman, 407–24. Chichester, UK: Wiley-Blackwell.

Geertz, Clifford. 1978. "The Bazaar Economy: Information and Search in Peasant Marketing." *American Economic Review* 68 (2): 28–32.

Goldthwaite, Richard A. 2009. *The Economy of Renaissance Florence*. Baltimore, MD: Johns Hopkins University Press.

Graeber, David. 2001. *Toward an Anthropological Theory of Value: The False Coin of Our Own Dreams*. New York: Palgrave.

———. 2005. "Value: Anthropological Theories of Value." In *A Handbook of Economic Anthropology*, edited by James G. Carrier, 439–54. Cheltenham, UK: Edward Elgar.

———. 2011. *Debt: The First 5,000 Years*. New York: Melville House.

Graham, Benjamin, and David L. Dodd. (1934) 1940. *Security Analysis: Principle and Technique*. 2nd ed. New York: McGraw-Hill.

"Greed Never Left." 2010. *Vanity Fair*, April 1. http://www.vanityfair.com/holly wood/2010/04/wall-street-201004.

Gregory, Chris. 2014. "On Religiosity and Commercial Life: Toward a Critique of Cultural Economy and Posthumanist Value Theory." *HAU: Journal of Ethnographic Theory* 4 (3): 45–68.

Grossman, Sanford J., and Joseph E. Stiglitz. 1980. "On the Impossibility of Informationally Efficient Markets." *American Economic Review* 70 (3): 393–408.

Guex, Sébastien. 2000. "The Origin of the Swiss Banking Secrecy Law and Its Repercussions for Swiss Federal Policy." *Business History Review* 74 (2): 237–66.

Guex, Sébastien, and Malik Mazbouri. 2010. "L'Historiographie des Banques et de la Place Financière Suisses aux 19e–20e Siècles." *Traverse: Revue d'Histoire* 17 (1): 203–28.

Guyer, Jane I. 2007. "Prophecy and the Near Future: Thoughts on Macroeconomic, Evangelical, and Punctuated Time." *American Ethnologist* 34 (3): 409–21.

Gumperz, John J., and Dell Hymes. 1986. *Directions in Sociolinguistics: The Ethnography of Communication*. Oxford, UK: Blackwell.

Hablützel, Peter. 2010. *Die Banken und Ihre Schweiz: Perspektiven einer Krise*. Zurich: Conzett and Oesch.

Hall, Peter A., and Rosemary C. R. Taylor. 1996. "Political Science and the Three New Institutionalisms." *Political Studies* 44 (5): 936–57.

Hann, Chris, and Keith Hart. 2009. "Introduction: Learning from Polanyi." In *Market and Society: The Great Transformation Today*, edited by Chris Hann and Keith Hart, 1–16. Cambridge: Cambridge University Press.

———. 2011. *Economic Anthropology: History, Ethnography, Critique*. Cambridge, UK: Polity.

Hansen, Kristian Bondo. 2015. "Contrarian Investment Philosophy in the American Stock Market: On Investment Advice and the Crowd Conundrum." *Economy and Society* 44 (4): 616–38.

Harrington, Brooke. 2016. *Capital without Borders: Wealth Managers and the One Percent*. Cambridge, MA: Harvard University Press.

Hart, Keith, and Horacio Ortiz. 2008. "Anthropology in the Financial Crisis." *Anthropology Today* 24 (6): 1–3.

Harvie, David, Geoff Lightfoot, and Kan Weir. 2013. "Ceux qui Font les Révolutions à Moitié ne Font que se Creuser un Tombeau." Paper presented at the Critical Management Studies Conference, Manchester, UK, July 10–12.

Hayek, Friedrich A. 1944. *The Road to Serfdom*. Chicago: University of Chicago Press.

———. 1945. "The Use of Knowledge in Society." *American Economic Review* 35 (4): 519–30.

———. 1960. *The Constitution of Liberty*. Chicago: University of Chicago Press.

Helgesson, Claes-Fredrik, and Fabian Muniesa. 2013. "For What It's Worth: An Introduction to Valuation Studies." *Valuation Studies* 1 (1): 1–10.

Hertz, Ellen. 1998. *The Trading Crowd: An Ethnography of the Shanghai Stock Market*. Cambridge: Cambridge University Press.

———. 2000. "Stock Markets as 'Simulacra': Observation That Participates." *Tsantsa* 5:40–50.

Hertz, Ellen, and Stefan Leins. 2012. "The 'Real Economy' and Its Pariahs: Questioning Moral Dichotomies in Contemporary Capitalism." Theorizing the Contemporary, *Cultural Anthropology* website, May 15. http://culanth.org/?q=node/576.

Hilgers, Mathieu. 2012. "The Historicity of the Neoliberal State." *Social Anthropology* 20 (1): 80–94.

Ho, Karen. 2005. "Situating Global Capitalisms: A View from Wall Street Investment Banks." *Cultural Anthropology* 20 (1): 68–96.

———. 2009. *Liquidated: An Ethnography of Wall Street*. Durham, NC: Duke University Press.

Hodson, Geoffrey M. 2006. "What Are Institutions?" *Journal of Economic Issues* 40 (1): 1–25.

Holmes, Douglas R. 2009. "Economy of Words." *Cultural Anthropology* 24 (3): 381–419.

———. 2014. *Economy of Words: Communicative Imperatives in Central Banks*. Chicago: University of Chicago Press.

Holmes, Douglas, and George Marcus. 2005. "Cultures of Expertise and the Management of Globalization: Toward the Re-Functioning of Ethnography." In *Global Assemblages: Technology, Politics, and Ethics as Anthropological Problems*, edited by Aihwa Ong and Stephen J. Collier, 235–52. Malden, MA: Blackwell.

"Investments: Orlando Is the Cat's Whiskers of Stock Picking." 2013. *Guardian*, January 13. http://www.theguardian.com/money/2013/jan/13/investments-stock-picking.

"Is This Really the End?" 2011. *Economist*, November 26. http://www.economist.com/printedition/2011-11-26.

Jensen, Michael C., and Clifford W. Smith Jr. 1984. "The Theory of Corporate Finance: A Historical Overview." In *The Modern Theory of Corporate Finance*, edited by Michael C. Jensen and Clifford W. Smith Jr., 2–20. New York: McGraw-Hill.

Jovanovic, Franck, and Philippe Le Gall. 2001. "Does God Practice a Random Walk? The 'Financial Physics' of a Nineteenth-Century Forerunner, Jules Regnault." *European Journal of the History of Economic Thought* 8 (3): 332–62.

Juris, Jeffrey S. 2012. "Reflections on #Occupy Everywhere: Social Media, Public Space, and Emerging Logics of Aggregation." *American Ethnologist* 39 (2): 259–79.

Kahneman, Daniel. 2011. *Thinking, Fast and Slow*. London: Penguin.

Kahneman, Daniel, and Amos Tversky. 1973. "On the Psychology of Prediction." *Psychological Review* 80 (4): 237–51.

———. 1979. "Prospect Theory: An Analysis of Decision under Risk." *Econometrica* 47 (2): 263–92.

Kanton Zürich. 2011, January. "Finanzplatz Zürich 2011: Monitoring, Prognosen, Perspektiven bis 2020. Eine Studie im Auftrag des Amtes fur Wirtschaft und Arbeit." http://www.awa.zh.ch/dam/volkswirtschaftsdirektion/awa/amt/veroeffentlichungen/BAK_2011_1.pdf.

Kendall, Maurice. 1953. "The Analysis of Economic Time Series, Part I: Prices." *Journal of the Royal Statistical Society* 116 (1): 11–34.

Keynes, John Maynard. 1936. *The General Theory of Employment, Interest and Money*. New York: Harcourt.

Knight, Frank H. 1921. *Risk, Uncertainty, and Profit*. Boston: Houghton Mifflin.

Knight, Jack. 1992. *Institutions and Social Conflict*. Cambridge: Cambridge University Press.

Knight, Jack, and Itai Sened. 1995. Introduction to *Explaining Social Institutions*, edited by Jack Knight and Itai Sened, 1–14. Ann Arbor: University of Michigan Press.

Knorr Cetina, Karin. 2007. "Culture in Global Knowledge Societies: Knowledge Cultures and Epistemic Cultures." *Interdisciplinary Science Reviews* 32 (4): 361–75.

———. 2010. "The Epistemics of Information: A Consumption Model." *Journal of Consumer Culture* 10 (2): 171–201.

———. 2011. "Financial Analysis: Epistemic Profile of an Evaluative Science." In *Social Knowledge in the Making*, edited by Charles Camic, Neil Gross, and Michèle Lamond, 405–41. Chicago: University of Chicago Press.

Latour, Bruno. 2013. *An Inquiry into Modes of Existence: An Anthropology of the Moderns*. Cambridge, MA: Harvard University Press.

Latour, Bruno, and Steve Woolgar. 1979. *Laboratory Life: The Social Construction of Scientific Facts*. London: Sage.

Lee, Frederic. 2009. *A History of Heterodox Economics: Challenging the Mainstream in the Twentieth Century*. London: Routledge.

Leins, Stefan. 2010. "Zur Ethik des islamischen Finanzmarktes." *Zeitschrift für Wirtschafts- und Unternehmensethik* 11 (1): 66–75.

———. 2011. "Pricing the Revolution: Financial Analysts Respond to the Egyptian Uprising." *Anthropology Today* 27 (4): 11–14.

———. 2013. "Playing the Market? The Role of Risk, Uncertainty and Authority in the Construction of Stock Market Forecasts." In *Qualitative Research in Gambling: Exploring the Production and Consumption of Risk*, edited by Rebecca Cassidy, Andrea Pisac, and Claire Loussouarn, 218–32. London: Routledge.

Lépinay, Vincent Antonin. 2011. *Codes of Finance: Engineering Derivatives in a Global Bank*. Princeton, NJ: Princeton University Press.

Lépinay, Vincent Antonin, and Ellen Hertz. 2005. "Deception and Its Preconditions: Issues Raised by Financial Markets." In *Deception in Markets: An Economic Analysis*, edited by Caroline Gerschlager, 267–300. Houndmills, UK: Palgrave Macmillan.

Lewis, Michael. 2014. *Flash Boys: A Wall Street Revolt*. New York: W. W. Norton.

LiPuma, Edward, and Benjamin Lee. 2004. *Financial Derivatives and the Globalization of Risk*. Durham, NC: Duke University Press.

Lo, Andrew W. 2008. "Efficient Market Hypothesis." In *The New Palgrave Dictionary of Economics*, 2nd ed., edited by Steven N. Durlauf and Lawrence E. Blume. http://www.dictionaryofeconomics.com/dictionary.

Loussouarn, Claire. 2010. "Buying Moments of Happiness: Luck, Time and Agency among Chinese Casino Players in London." PhD diss., Goldsmiths, University of London.

Luhmann, Niklas. 1998. *Observations on Modernity*. Stanford, CA: Stanford University Press.

———. 2000. *Art as a Social System*. Stanford, CA: Stanford University Press.

MacKenzie, Donald. 2006. *An Engine, Not a Camera: How Financial Models Shape Markets*. Cambridge, MA: MIT Press.

MacKenzie, Donald, Daniel Beunza, Yuval Millo, and Juan Pablo Pardo-Guerra. 2012. "Drilling through the Allegheny Mountains: Liquidity, Materiality and High-Frequency Trading." *Journal of Cultural Economy* 5 (3): 279–96.

MacKenzie, Donald, and Yuval Millo. 2003. "Constructing a Market, Performing Theory: The Historical Sociology of a Financial Derivatives Exchange." *American Journal of Sociology* 109 (1): 107–45.

MacKenzie, Donald, Fabian Muniesa, and Lucia Siu, eds. 2007. *Do Economists Make Markets? On the Performativity of Economics*. Princeton, NJ: Princeton University Press.

Maggio, Rodolfo. 2014. "The Anthropology of Storytelling and the Storytelling of Anthropology." *Journal of Comparative Research in Anthropology and Sociology* 5 (2): 89–106.

Malkiel, Burton. (1973) 1985. *A Random Walk down Wall Street*. 4th ed. New York: W. W. Norton.

Mankiw, N. Gregory. 2015. *Principles of Economics*. 7th ed. Stanford, CT: Cengage Learning.

Mars, Frank. 1998. "'Wir sind alle Seher': Die Praxis der Aktienanalyse." PhD diss., University of Bielefeld.

Marti, Emilio, and Andreas Georg Scherer. 2016. "Financial Regulation and

Social Welfare: The Critical Contribution of Management Theory." *Academy of Management Review* 41 (2): 298–323.

Marx, Karl. (1867) 1990. *Capital: A Critique of Political Economy*, vol. 1. London: Penguin.

Mason, Arthur, and Maria Stoilkova. 2012. "Corporeality of Consultant Expertise in Arctic Natural Gas Development." *Journal of Northern Studies* 6 (2): 83–96.

Maurer, Bill. 2002. "Repressed Futures: Financial Derivatives' Theological Unconscious." *Economy and Society* 31 (1): 15–36.

———. 2005. *Mutual Life, Limited: Islamic Banking, Alternative Currencies, Lateral Reason*. Princeton, NJ: Princeton University Press.

Mauss, Marcel. (1923) 2002. *The Gift: The Form and Reason for Exchange in Archaic Societies*. London: Routledge.

Merton, Robert K. 1948. "The Self-Fulfilling Prophecy." *Antioch Review* 8 (2): 193–210.

Michaely, Roni, and Kent L. Womack. 2005. "Market Efficiency and Biases in Brokerage Recommendations." In *Advances in Behavioral Finance*, vol. 2, edited by Richard H. Thaler, 389–419. Princeton, NJ: Princeton University Press.

Miller, Daniel. 2002. Turning Callon the Right Way Up. *Economy and Society* 31 (2): 218–33.

Miller, H. Laurence. 1962. "On the 'Chicago School of Economics.'" *Journal of Political Economy* 70 (1): 64–69.

Mirowski, Philip, and Edward Nik-Khah. 2007. "Markets Made Flesh: Performativity, and a Problem in Science Studies, Augmented with Consideration of the FCC Auctions." In *Do Economists Make Markets? On the Performativity of Economics*, edited by Donald MacKenzie, Fabian Muniesa, and Lucia Siu, 190–224. Princeton, NJ: Princeton University Press.

Mirowski, Philip, and Dieter Plehwe. 2009. *The Road from Mont Pèlerin: The Making of the Neoliberal Thought Collective*. Cambridge, MA: Harvard University Press.

Miyazaki, Hirokazu. 2003. "The Temporalities of the Market." *American Anthropologist* 105 (2): 255–65.

———. 2007. "Between Arbitrage and Speculation: An Economy of Belief and Doubt." *Economy and Society* 36 (3): 396–415.

———. 2013. *Arbitraging Japan: Dreams of Capitalism at the End of Finance*. Berkeley, CA: University of California Press.

Moebius, Stephan, and Markus Schroer. 2010. Introduction to *Diven, Hacker, Spekulanten: Sozialfiguren der Gegenwart*, edited by Stephan Moebius and Markus Schroer, 7–11. Frankfurt am Main: Suhrkamp.

Montier, James. 2002. *Behavioral Finance: Insights into Irrational Minds and Markets*. Chichester, UK: Wiley.

MSCI. 2012, March 2. "GICS Structure." http://www.msci.com/resources/pdfs /MK-GICS-DIR-3-02.pdf.

Muniesa, Fabian. 2008. "Trading-Room Telephones and the Identification of

Counterparts." In *Living in a Material World: Economic Sociology Meets Science and Technology Studies*, edited by Trevor Pinch and Richard Swedberg, 291–313. Cambridge, MA: MIT Press.

———. 2011. "Comment la Bourse Fait ses Prix: Ethnographie d'un Cours d'Action Boursière." In *Humains, Non-Humains: Comment Repeupler les Sciences Sociales*, edited by Sophie Houdart and Olivier Thiery, 176–90. Paris: Presses Universitaires de France.

———. 2014. *The Provoked Economy: Economic Reality and the Performative Turn*. London: Routledge.

North, Douglass C. 1990. *Institutions, Institutional Change and Economic Performance*. Cambridge: Cambridge University Press.

———. 1992. "Institutions and Economic Theory." *American Economist* 36 (1): 3–6.

"On the Edge." 2011. *Economist*, July 16. http://www.economist.com/printedition /2011-07-16.

Ortiz, Horacio. "Financial value: Economic, moral, political, global." *HAU: Journal of Ethnographic Theory* 3 (1): 64–79.

Osborne, Matthew F. M. 1959. "Brownian Motion in the Stock Market." *Operations Research* 7 (2): 145–73.

Pardo-Guerra, Juan Pablo. 2012. "Financial Automation, Past, Present and Future." In *Oxford Handbook of the Sociology of Finance*, edited by Karin Knorr-Cetina and Alex Preda, 567–86. Oxford, UK: Oxford University Press.

Perrenoud, Marc, Rodrigo López, Florian Adank, Jan Baumann, Alain Cortat, and Suzanne Peters. 2002. *La Place Financière et les Banques Suisses à l'Epoque du National-Socialisme: Les Relations des Grandes Banques avec l'Allemagne (1931–1946)*. Veröffentlichungen der UEK, Band 13. Zurich: Chronos.

Polanyi, Karl. (1944) 1957. *The Great Transformation: The Political and Economic Origins of Our Time*. Boston: Beacon Press.

Polanyi, Michael. (1966) 2009. *The Tacit Dimension*. Chicago: University of Chicago Press.

Posamentier, Alfred S., and Ingmar Lehmann. 2007. *The Fabulous Fibonacci Numbers*. New York: Prometheus.

Power, Michael. 2012. "Accounting and Finance." In *The Oxford Handbook of Sociology of Finance*, edited by Karin Knorr Cetina and Alex Preda, 293–316. Oxford, UK: Oxford University Press.

Preda, Alex. 2002. "Financial Knowledge, Documents, and the Structures of Financial Activities." *Journal of Contemporary Ethnography* 31 (2): 207–39.

———. 2004. "Informative Prices, Rational Investors: The Emergence of the Random Walk Hypothesis and the Nineteenth-Century 'Science of Financial Investments.'" *History of Political Economy* 36 (2): 351–86.

———. 2007. "Where Do Analysts Come From? The Case of Financial Chartism." In *Market Devices*, edited by Michel Callon, Yuval Millo, and Fabian Muniesa, 40–64. Malden, MA: Blackwell.

———. 2009. *Framing Finance: The Boundaries of Markets and Modern Capitalism*. Chicago: University of Chicago Press.

Rabinow, Paul. 2008. *Marking Time: On the Anthropology of the Contemporary*. Princeton, NJ: Princeton University Press.

Rajak, Dinah. 2011. *In Good Company: An Anatomy of Corporate Social Responsibility*. Stanford, CA: Stanford University Press.

Rankin, Katharine N., and Yogendra B. Shakya. 2007. "Neoliberalizing the Grassroots? Microfinance and the Politics of Development in Nepal." In *Neoliberalization: States, Networks, Peoples*, edited by Kim England and Kevin Ward, 48–76. Malden, MA: Blackwell.

Richard, Analiese, and Daromir Rudnyckyj. 2009. "Economies of Affect." *Journal of the Royal Anthropological Institute* 15 (1): 57–77.

Riles, Annelise. 2004. "Real Time: Unwinding Technocratic and Anthropological Knowledge." *American Ethnologist* 31 (3): 392–405.

———. 2006. Introduction to *Documents: Artifacts of modern knowledge*, edited by Annelise Riles, 1–38. Ann Arbor: University of Michigan Press.

———. 2010. "Collateral Expertise: Legal Knowledge in the Global Financial Markets." *Current Anthropology* 51 (6): 795–818.

———. 2011. *Collateral Knowledge: Legal Reasoning in the Global Financial Markets*. Chicago: University of Chicago Press.

Ritzmann, Franz. 1973. *Die Schweizer Banken: Geschichte—Theorie—Statistik*. Bern, Switz.: Paul Haupt.

Roose, Kevin. 2014. *Young Money: Inside the Hidden World of Wall Street's Post-Crash Recruits*. New York: Grand Central.

Rudnyckyj, Daromir. 2010. *Spiritual Economies: Islam, Globalization, and the Afterlife of Development*. Ithaca, NY: Cornell University Press.

Samir, dir. 2005. *Snow White* [movie]. Zurich: Dschoint Ventschr Filmproduktion.

Samuelson, Paul. 1965. "Proof That Properly Anticipated Prices Fluctuate Randomly." *Industrial Management Review* 6 (2): 41–49.

Schumpeter, Joseph A. (1911) 2012. *The Theory of Economic Development: An Inquiry into Profits, Capital, Credit, Interest, and the Business Cycle*. New Brunswick, NJ: Transaction.

Sen, Falguni, and Michael Shiel. 2006. "From Business Process Outsourcing (BPO) to Knowledge Process Outsourcing (KPO): Some Issues." *Human Systems Management* 25 (2): 145–55.

Shefrin, Hersh. 2000. *Beyond Greed and Fear: Understanding Behavioral Finance and the Psychology of Investing*. Boston: Harvard Business School Press.

Shiller, Robert J. 2017. "Narrative Economics." Cowles Foundation Discussion Paper No. 2069. https://ssrn.com/abstract=2896857.

"Shoot All the Analysts." 2001. *Financial Times*, March 19.

Shouse, Eric. 2005. "Feeling, Emotion, Affect." *M/C Journal* 8 (6). http://journal.media-culture.org.au/0512/03-shouse.php.

Simon, Herbert A. 1957. *Models of Man: Social and Rational; Mathematical Essays on Rational Human Behavior in a Social Setting.* New York: Wiley.

Smith, Adam. (1759) 2002. *The Theory of Moral Sentiments.* Cambridge: Cambridge University Press.

———. (1776) 1991. *An Inquiry into the Nature and Causes of the Wealth of Nations.* Amherst, NY: Prometheus.

Smith, Philip, and Eric Thurman. 2007. *A Billion Bootstraps: Microcredit, Barefoot Banking, and the Business Solution for Ending Poverty.* New York: McGraw-Hill.

Stäheli, Urs. 2010. "Der Spekulant." In *Diven, Hacker, Spekulanten: Sozialfiguren der Gegenwart,* edited by Stephan Moebius and Markus Schroer, 353–65. Frankfurt am Main: Suhrkamp.

Stark, David. 2009. *The Sense of Dissonance: Accounts of Worth in Economic Life.* Princeton, NJ: Princeton University Press.

Stark, David, and Daniel Beunza. 2009. "The Cognitive Ecology of an Arbitrage Trading Room." In *The Sense of Dissonance: Accounts of Worth in Economic Life,* edited by David Stark, 118–62. Princeton, NJ: Princeton University Press.

Stehr, Nico. 2008. *Moral Markets: How Knowledge and Affluence Change Consumers and Products.* Boulder, CO: Paradigm.

"Stock Market Becomes Short Attention Span Theater of Trading." 2011. *Forbes,* January 21. http://www.forbes.com/sites/greatspeculations/2011/01/21 /stock-market-becomes-short-attention-span-theater-of-trading/.

Strange, Susan. 1986. *Casino Capitalism.* Oxford: Blackwell.

Strathern, Marilyn. 2000. "Introduction: New Accountabilities." In *Audit Cultures: Anthropological Studies in Accountability, Ethics and the Academy,* edited by Marilyn Strathern, 1–18. London: Routledge.

Straumann, Tobias. 2006. "Der kleine Gigant: Der Aufstieg Zürichs zu einem internationalen Finanzplatz." In *Europäische Finanzplätze im Wettbewerb,* edited by Institut für bankhistorische Forschung, 139–69. Stuttgart: Franz Steiner.

———. 2010. "The UBS Crisis in Historical Perspective. Expert Opinion, Prepared for the Delivery to UBS AG, 28 September 2010." Working Paper, Institute for Empirical Research in Economics, University of Zurich.

Swiss Bankers Association. 2008, January. *Directives on the Independence of Financial Research.* January. http://shop.sba.ch/12108_d.pdf.

Swiss Federal Council. 1934, February 2. "Botschaft des Bundesrates an die Bundesversammlung betreffend den Entwurf eines Bundesgesetzes über die Banken und Sparkassen." http://www.amtsdruckschriften.bar.admin.ch /viewOrigDoc.do?ID=10032224.

Tanner, Jakob. 1993. "Die Entwicklung des schweizerischen Finanzplatzes: Fragestellungen und Problemfelder." In *Banken und Kredit in der Schweiz (1850–1930),* edited by Youssef Cassis and Jakob Tanner, 21–28. Zurich: Chronos.

———. 1997. "Die internationalen Finanzbeziehungen der Schweiz zwischen 1931 und 1950." *Schweizerische Zeitschrift für Geschichte* 47 (4): 492–519.

————. 2016. "Narratives." In *Protest Cultures: A Companion*, edited by Kathrin Fahlenbrach, Martin Klimke, and Joachim Scharloth, 137–45. New York: Berghahn.

"10 Questions for Daniel Kahneman: Psychologist and Nobel-Winning Economist Daniel Kahneman on Why People Don't Make Rational Choices." 2011. *Time*, November 28. http://content.time.com/time/magazine/article/0,9171 ,2099712,00.html.

Thrift, Nigel. 2005. *Knowing Capitalism*. London: Sage.

Turner, Victor. 1975. *Revelation and Divination in Ndembu Ritual*. Ithaca, NY: Cornell University Press.

Valdez, Stephen. 2007. *An Introduction to Global Financial Markets*. 5th ed. New York: Palgrave Macmillan.

Van Horn, Robert, and Philipp Mirowski. 2010. "Neoliberalism and Chicago." In *The Elgar Companion to the Chicago School of Economics*, edited by Ross B. Emmett, 196–206. Cheltenham, UK: Edward Elgar.

Van Overtveldt, Johan. 2007. *The Chicago School: How the University of Chicago Assembled the Thinkers Who Revolutionized Economics and Business*. Chicago: Agate.

Veblen, Thorstein. (1899) 2007. *The Theory of the Leisure Class: An Economic Study of Institutions*. Oxford, UK: Oxford University Press.

"Vorwärts nach Zürich Paradeplatz." 2011. WOZ, October 13.

Wacquant, Loïc. 2012. "Three Steps to a Historical Anthropology of Actually Existing Neoliberalism." *Social Anthropology* 20 (1): 66–79.

Wansleben, Leon. 2012. "Financial Analysts." In *The Oxford Handbook of the Sociology of Finance*, edited by Karin Knorr Cetina and Alex Preda, 250–71. Oxford, UK: Oxford University Press.

————. 2013a. *Cultures of Expertise in Global Currency Markets*. London: Routledge.

————. 2013b. "Dreaming with BRICs: Innovating the Classificatory Regimes of International Finance." *Journal of Cultural Economy* 6 (4): 453–71.

Weber, Max. (1905) 2009. *The Protestant Ethic and the Spirit of Capitalism*. Oxford, UK: Oxford University Press.

Wetzel, Dietmar J., Markus Flück, and Lukas Hofstätter. 2010. "Konturen einer Branche im Umbruch: Das Bankenfeld in Deutschland, Österreich und der Schweiz." In *Strukturierte Verantwortungslosigkeit: Berichte aus der Bankenwelt*, edited by Claudia Honegger, Sighard Neckel, and Chantal Magnin, 335–70. Berlin: Suhrkamp.

"Why Are Swiss Bankers Called Gnomes?" 2010. BBC, February 25. http://news .bbc.co.uk/2/hi/uk_news/magazine/8534936.stm.

"The Wisdom of Exercising Patience in Investing." 2012. Reuters, March 2. http://www.reuters.com/article/us-patience-saft-idUSTRE8210O6201 20302.

"Woher das Schwarzgeld auf Schweizer Banken kommt." 2010. *Tages-Anzeiger*. February 12.

Working, Holbrook. 1934. "A Random Difference Series for Use in the Analysis of Time Series." *Journal of the American Statistical Association* 29 (185): 11–24.

Zaloom, Caitlin. 2003. "Ambiguous Numbers: Trading Technologies and Interpretation in Financial Markets." *American Ethnologist* 30 (2): 258–72.

———. 2004. "The Productive Life of Risk." *Cultural Anthropology* 19 (3): 365–91.

———. 2006. *Out of the Pits: Trading Technologies from Chicago to London.* Chicago: University of Chicago Press.

———. 2009. "How to Read the Future: The Yield Curve, Affect, and Financial Prediction." *Public Culture* 21 (2): 245–68.

Zigon, Jarrett. 2012. "Narratives." In *A Companion to Moral Anthropology*, edited by Didier Fassin, 204–20. Chichester: Wiley-Blackwell.

Zuckerman, Ezra W. 1999. "The Categorical Imperative: Securities Analysts and the Illegitimacy Discount." *American Journal of Sociology* 104 (5): 1398–1438.

———. 2012. "Market Efficiency: A Sociological Perspective." In *The Oxford Handbook of the Sociology of Finance*, edited by Karin Knorr Cetina and Alex Preda, 223–49. Oxford, UK: Oxford University Press.

Zucman, Gabriel. 2016. *The Hidden Wealth of Nations: The Scourge of Tax Havens.* Chicago: University of Chicago Press.

Index

Page numbers in italics refer to figures and tables.